Volleyball Scorebook

Book Holder: ....

Team: ....

We Love to Hear Your Voice
You Can do That by Leaving a Review for Our Book

Thank You For Your Purchase !

Date: Home: Visitor: Set #:

Time-Outs					First Serve (Check Box Below)		Time-Outs			
		Game No:								

Serve Order	Player No	Team:											L:		1 16	1 16	Serve Order	Player No	Team:										L:
I															2 17	2 17	I											
II															3 18 4 19	3 18 4 19	II											
III															5 20 6 21 7 22	5 20 6 21 7 22	III											
IV															8 23 9 24 10 25	8 23 9 24 10 25	IV											
V															11 26 12 27 13 28	11 26 12 27 13 28	V											
VI															14 29 15 30	14 29 15 30	VI											
									Final Score:														Official Verification				

Subs: 1 2 3 4 5 6 7 8 9 10 11 12 13 14 15 16 17 18   Subs: 1 2 3 4 5 6 7 8 9 10 11 12 13 14 15 16 17 18

Comments: ....   Comments: ....

Referee: ....   Umpire: ....

Scorekeeper: ....

Key:
- C=Playing Captain
- P-1=Penalty Point
- T= Time-out
- 1=Point
- P=Penalty
- TX=Time-out Opponent
- ⊣ =Loss of Rally
- Px=Penalty Opponent
- S=Substitution Serving Team
- ☐ =Point Scored Off Loss of Rally
- R=Reply
- Sx=Opponent Substitution
- △ =Libero Point
- Rs=Re-Serve

If the receiving team wins the rally, it receives a point which is recorded on the line of the NEXT server's a number and a square is drawn around it. Also draw a square around the same point on the team's running score.

Date: Home: Visitor: Set #:

Time-Outs		Game No:		First Serve (Check Box Below)		Time-Outs			

Serve Order	Player No	Team: L:						Serve Order	Player No	Team: L:	
I				1 16	1 16			I			
				2 17	2 17						
II				3 18	3 18			II			
				4 19	4 19						
				5 20	5 20						
III				6 21	6 21			III			
				7 22	7 22						
				8 23	8 23						
IV				9 24	9 24			IV			
				10 25	10 25						
V				11 26	11 26			V			
				12 27	12 27						
				13 28	13 28						
VI				14 29	14 29			VI			
				15 30	15 30						
		Final Score:								Official Verification	

Subs: 1 2 3 4 5 6 7 8 9 10 11 12 13 14 15 16 17 18   Subs: 1 2 3 4 5 6 7 8 9 10 11 12 13 14 15 16 17 18

Comments: ....   Comments: ....

Referee: ....   Umpire: ....

Scorekeeper: ....

Key:

C=Playing Captain	1=Point	⌐=Loss of Rally	☐ =Point Scored Off Loss of Rally	△ =Libero Point
P-1=Penalty Point	P=Penalty	Px=Penalty Opponent	R=Reply	Rs=Re-Serve
T= Time-out	TX=Time-out Opponent	S=Substitution Serving Team	Sx=Opponent Substitution	

If the receiving team wins the rally, it receives a point which is recorded on the line of the NEXT server's
a number and a square is drawn around it. Also draw a square around the same point on the team's running score.

Date: _____ Home: _____ Visitor: _____ Set #: _____

Time-Outs		Game No:			First Serve (Check Box Below)		Time-Outs			

Serve Order	Player No	Team:		L:				Serve Order	Player No	Team:		L:
I						1 16 / 1 16		I				
						2 17 / 2 17						
II						3 18 / 3 18		II				
						4 19 / 4 19						
						5 20 / 5 20						
III						6 21 / 6 21		III				
						7 22 / 7 22						
						8 23 / 8 23						
IV						9 24 / 9 24		IV				
						10 25 / 10 25						
V						11 26 / 11 26		V				
						12 27 / 12 27						
						13 28 / 13 28						
VI						14 29 / 14 29		VI				
						15 30 / 15 30						

Final Score: _____   Official Verification _____

Subs: 1 2 3 4 5 6 7 8 9 10 11 12 13 14 15 16 17 18   Subs: 1 2 3 4 5 6 7 8 9 10 11 12 13 14 15 16 17 18

Comments: ....   Comments: ....

Referee: ....   Umpire: ....

Scorekeeper: ....

Key:

C=Playing Captain	1=Point	⊣ =Loss of Rally	☐ =Point Scored Off Loss of Rally	△ =Libero Point
P-1=Penalty Point	P=Penalty	Px=Penalty Opponent	R=Reply	Rs=Re-Serve
T= Time-out	TX=Time-out Opponent	S=Substitution Serving Team	Sx=Opponent Substitution	

If the receiving team wins the rally, it receives a point which is recorded on the line of the NEXT server's
a number and a square is drawn around it. Also draw a square around the same point on the team's running score.

Date: Home: Visitor: Set #:

Time-Outs		Game No:			First Serve (Check Box Below)		Time-Outs			

Serve Order	Player No	Team:		L:			Serve Order	Player No	Team:		L:
I						1 16 1 16 2 17 2 17	I				
II						3 18 3 18 4 19 4 19 5 20 5 20	II				
III						6 21 6 21 7 22 7 22	III				
IV						8 23 8 23 9 24 9 24 10 25 10 25	IV				
V						11 26 11 26 12 27 12 27 13 28 13 28	V				
VI						14 29 14 29 15 30 15 30	VI				

Final Score: Official Verification

Subs: 1 2 3 4 5 6 7 8 9 10 11 12 13 14 15 16 17 18   Subs: 1 2 3 4 5 6 7 8 9 10 11 12 13 14 15 16 17 18

Comments: Comments:

Referee: Umpire:

Scorekeeper:

Key:

C=Playing Captain	1=Point	⊣ =Loss of Rally	☐ =Point Scored Off Loss of Rally	△ =Libero Point
P-1=Penalty Point	P=Penalty	Px=Penalty Opponent	R=Reply	Rs=Re-Serve
T= Time-out	TX=Time-out Opponent	S=Substitution Serving Team	Sx=Opponent Substitution	

If the receiving team wins the rally, it receives a point which is recorded on the line of the NEXT server's
a number and a square is drawn around it. Also draw a square around the same point on the team's running score.

Date: Home: Visitor: Set #:

Time-Outs		Game No:			First Serve (Check Box Below)		Time-Outs			
Serve Order	**Player No**	**Team:**	**L:**				**Serve Order**	**Player No**	**Team:**	**L:**
I					1 16 / 2 17	1 16 / 2 17	I			
II					3 18 / 4 19 / 5 20	3 18 / 4 19 / 5 20	II			
III					6 21 / 7 22	6 21 / 7 22	III			
IV					8 23 / 9 24 / 10 25	8 23 / 9 24 / 10 25	IV			
V					11 26 / 12 27 / 13 28	11 26 / 12 27 / 13 28	V			
VI					14 29 / 15 30	14 29 / 15 30	VI			
			Final Score:						Official Verification	

Subs: 1 2 3 4 5 6 7 8 9 10 11 12 13 14 15 16 17 18   Subs: 1 2 3 4 5 6 7 8 9 10 11 12 13 14 15 16 17 18

Comments: ....   Comments: ....

Referee: ....   Umpire: ....

Scorekeeper: ....

Key:
C=Playing Captain	1=Point	⊣ =Loss of Rally	☐ =Point Scored Off Loss of Rally	△ =Libero Point
P-1=Penalty Point	P=Penalty	Px=Penalty Opponent	R=Reply	Rs=Re-Serve
T= Time-out	TX=Time-out Opponent	S=Substitution Serving Team	Sx=Opponent Substitution	

If the receiving team wins the rally, it receives a point which is recorded on the line of the NEXT server's
a number and a square is drawn around it. Also draw a square around the same point on the team's running score.

Date:	Home:	Visitor:	Set #:

Time-Outs		Game No:		First Serve (Check Box Below)		Time-Outs		

Serve Order	Player No	Team:								L:								Serve Order	Player No	Team:									L:						

Middle column serve/point numbers:

I	1 16 — 1 16	I
	2 17 — 2 17	
II	3 18 — 3 18	II
	4 19 — 4 19	
	5 20 — 5 20	
III	6 21 — 6 21	III
	7 22 — 7 22	
	8 23 — 8 23	
IV	9 24 — 9 24	IV
	10 25 — 10 25	
V	11 26 — 11 26	V
	12 27 — 12 27	
	13 28 — 13 28	
VI	14 29 — 14 29	VI
	15 30 — 15 30	

Final Score:

Official Verification

Subs: 1 2 3 4 5 6 7 8 9 10 11 12 13 14 15 16 17 18

Subs: 1 2 3 4 5 6 7 8 9 10 11 12 13 14 15 16 17 18

Comments: ....

Comments: ....

Referee: ....

Umpire: ....

Scorekeeper: ....

Key:

C=Playing Captain	1=Point	⊣ =Loss of Rally	☐ =Point Scored Off Loss of Rally	△ =Libero Point
P-1=Penalty Point	P=Penalty	Px=Penalty Opponent	R=Reply	Rs=Re-Serve
T= Time-out	TX=Time-out Opponent	S=Substitution Serving Team	Sx=Opponent Substitution	

If the receiving team wins the rally, it receives a point which is recorded on the line of the NEXT server's
a number and a square is drawn around it. Also draw a square around the same point on the team's running score.

Date: _____ Home: _____ Visitor: _____ Set #: _____

Time-Outs		Game No:				First Serve (Check Box Below)		Time-Outs		Team:		L:	

Serve Order	Player No	Team:												L:			First Serve		Serve Order	Player No	Team:												L:		

| | | | | | | | | | | | | | | | | | 1 16 / 1 16 | | | | | | | | | | | | | | | | | | |

Serve Order (left): I, II, III, IV, V, VI

First Serve (Check Box Below) columns:

1 16	1 16
2 17	2 17
3 18	3 18
4 19	4 19
5 20	5 20
6 21	6 21
7 22	7 22
8 23	8 23
9 24	9 24
10 25	10 25
11 26	11 26
12 27	12 27
13 28	13 28
14 29	14 29
15 30	15 30

Serve Order (right): I, II, III, IV, V, VI

Final Score: _____   Official Verification _____

Subs: 1 2 3 4 5 6 7 8 9 10 11 12 13 14 15 16 17 18   Subs: 1 2 3 4 5 6 7 8 9 10 11 12 13 14 15 16 17 18

Comments: ....   Comments: ....

Referee: ....   Umpire: ....

Scorekeeper: ....

Key:

C=Playing Captain	1=Point	⊣ =Loss of Rally	☐ =Point Scored Off Loss of Rally	△ =Libero Point
P-1=Penalty Point	P=Penalty	Px=Penalty Opponent	R=Reply	Rs=Re-Serve
T= Time-out	TX=Time-out Opponent	S=Substitution Serving Team	Sx=Opponent Substitution	

If the receiving team wins the rally, it receives a point which is recorded on the line of the NEXT server's
a number and a square is drawn around it. Also draw a square around the same point on the team's running score.

Date: Home: Visitor: Set #:

Time-Outs		Game No:			First Serve (Check Box Below)		Time-Outs			

Serve Order	Player No	Team:										L:							Serve Order	Player No	Team:								L:
I														1 16	1 16	I												
II														2 17 / 3 18	2 17 / 3 18	II												
III														4 19 / 5 20 / 6 21	4 19 / 5 20 / 6 21	III												
IV														7 22 / 8 23 / 9 24	7 22 / 8 23 / 9 24	IV												
V														10 25 / 11 26 / 12 27 / 13 28	10 25 / 11 26 / 12 27 / 13 28	V												
VI														14 29 / 15 30	14 29 / 15 30	VI												
								Final Score:										Official Verification		

Subs: 1 2 3 4 5 6 7 8 9 10 11 12 13 14 15 16 17 18   Subs: 1 2 3 4 5 6 7 8 9 10 11 12 13 14 15 16 17 18

Comments: ....   Comments: ....

....

Referee: ....   Umpire: ....

Scorekeeper: ....

Key:

C=Playing Captain	1=Point	⊣ =Loss of Rally	☐ =Point Scored Off Loss of Rally	△ =Libero Point
P-1=Penalty Point	P=Penalty	Px=Penalty Opponent	R=Reply	Rs=Re-Serve
T= Time-out	TX=Time-out Opponent	S=Substitution Serving Team	Sx=Opponent Substitution	

If the receiving team wins the rally, it receives a point which is recorded on the line of the NEXT server's
a number and a square is drawn around it. Also draw a square around the same point on the team's running score.

Date: _____ Home: _____ Visitor: _____ Set #: _____

Time-Outs		Game No:		First Serve (Check Box Below)		Time-Outs			

<table>
<tr><td colspan="2">Serve Order</td><td>Player No</td><td colspan="7">Team: L:</td><td></td><td></td><td>Serve Order</td><td>Player No</td><td colspan="7">Team: L:</td></tr>
<tr><td colspan="2">I</td><td></td><td colspan="7"></td><td>1 16
2 17</td><td>1 16
2 17</td><td>I</td><td></td><td colspan="7"></td></tr>
<tr><td colspan="2">II</td><td></td><td colspan="7"></td><td>3 18
4 19
5 20</td><td>3 18
4 19
5 20</td><td>II</td><td></td><td colspan="7"></td></tr>
<tr><td colspan="2">III</td><td></td><td colspan="7"></td><td>6 21
7 22</td><td>6 21
7 22</td><td>III</td><td></td><td colspan="7"></td></tr>
<tr><td colspan="2">IV</td><td></td><td colspan="7"></td><td>8 23
9 24
10 25</td><td>8 23
9 24
10 25</td><td>IV</td><td></td><td colspan="7"></td></tr>
<tr><td colspan="2">V</td><td></td><td colspan="7"></td><td>11 26
12 27
13 28</td><td>11 26
12 27
13 28</td><td>V</td><td></td><td colspan="7"></td></tr>
<tr><td colspan="2">VI</td><td></td><td colspan="7"></td><td>14 29
15 30</td><td>14 29
15 30</td><td>VI</td><td></td><td colspan="7"></td></tr>
<tr><td colspan="9">Final Score:</td><td></td><td></td><td colspan="9">Official Verification</td></tr>
</table>

Subs: 1 2 3 4 5 6 7 8 9 10 11 12 13 14 15 16 17 18   Subs: 1 2 3 4 5 6 7 8 9 10 11 12 13 14 15 16 17 18

Comments: ....   Comments: ....

Referee: ....   Umpire: ....

Scorekeeper: ....

Key:

C=Playing Captain	1=Point	⊣ =Loss of Rally	□ =Point Scored Off Loss of Rally	△ =Libero Point
P-1=Penalty Point	P=Penalty	Px=Penalty Opponent	R=Reply	Rs=Re-Serve
T= Time-out	TX=Time-out Opponent	S=Substitution Serving Team	Sx=Opponent Substitution	

If the receiving team wins the rally, it receives a point which is recorded on the line of the NEXT server's
a number and a square is drawn around it. Also draw a square around the same point on the team's running score.

Date: Home: Visitor: Set #:

Time-Outs		Game No:			First Serve (Check Box Below)		Time-Outs			

Serve Order	Player No	Team:									L:			Serve Order	Player No	Team:									L:	
I													1 16 / 2 17	I												
II													3 18 / 4 19 / 5 20	II												
III													6 21 / 7 22	III												
IV													8 23 / 9 24 / 10 25	IV												
V													11 26 / 12 27 / 13 28	V												
VI													14 29 / 15 30	VI												

First Serve check box numbers (left and right columns):
1 16   1 16
2 17   2 17
3 18   3 18
4 19   4 19
5 20   5 20
6 21   6 21
7 22   7 22
8 23   8 23
9 24   9 24
10 25   10 25
11 26   11 26
12 27   12 27
13 28   13 28
14 29   14 29
15 30   15 30

Final Score: Official Verification

Subs: 1 2 3 4 5 6 7 8 9 10 11 12 13 14 15 16 17 18   Subs: 1 2 3 4 5 6 7 8 9 10 11 12 13 14 15 16 17 18

Comments: ....   Comments: ....

Referee: ....   Umpire: ....

Scorekeeper: ....

Key:

C=Playing Captain	1=Point	⊣ =Loss of Rally	☐ =Point Scored Off Loss of Rally	△ =Libero Point
P-1=Penalty Point	P=Penalty	Px=Penalty Opponent	R=Reply	Rs=Re-Serve
T= Time-out	TX=Time-out Opponent	S=Substitution Serving Team	Sx=Opponent Substitution	

If the receiving team wins the rally, it receives a point which is recorded on the line of the NEXT server's
a number and a square is drawn around it. Also draw a square around the same point on the team's running score.

Date: Home: Visitor: Set #:

Time-Outs		Game No:			First Serve (Check Box Below)		Time-Outs			

Serve Order	Player No	Team:	L:				Serve Order	Player No	Team:	L:
I					1 16 / 2 17	1 16 / 2 17	I			
II					3 18 / 4 19 / 5 20	3 18 / 4 19 / 5 20	II			
III					6 21 / 7 22	6 21 / 7 22	III			
IV					8 23 / 9 24 / 10 25	8 23 / 9 24 / 10 25	IV			
V					11 26 / 12 27 / 13 28	11 26 / 12 27 / 13 28	V			
VI					14 29 / 15 30	14 29 / 15 30	VI			
			Final Score:						Official Verification	

Subs: 1 2 3 4 5 6 7 8 9 10 11 12 13 14 15 16 17 18   Subs: 1 2 3 4 5 6 7 8 9 10 11 12 13 14 15 16 17 18

Comments: ....   Comments: ....

Referee: ....   Umpire: ....

Scorekeeper: ....

Key:

C=Playing Captain	1=Point	⊣ =Loss of Rally	☐ =Point Scored Off Loss of Rally	△ =Libero Point
P-1=Penalty Point	P=Penalty	Px=Penalty Opponent	R=Reply	Rs=Re-Serve
T= Time-out	TX=Time-out Opponent	S=Substitution Serving Team	Sx=Opponent Substitution	

If the receiving team wins the rally, it receives a point which is recorded on the line of the NEXT server's a number and a square is drawn around it. Also draw a square around the same point on the team's running score.

Date: Home: Visitor: Set #:

	Time-Outs		Game No:			First Serve (Check Box Below)			Time-Outs			
Serve Order	Player No	Team:		L:				Serve Order	Player No	Team:		L:
I						1 16 / 2 17	1 16 / 2 17	I				
II						3 18 / 4 19 / 5 20	3 18 / 4 19 / 5 20	II				
III						6 21 / 7 22	6 21 / 7 22	III				
IV						8 23 / 9 24 / 10 25	8 23 / 9 24 / 10 25	IV				
V						11 26 / 12 27	11 26 / 12 27	V				
VI						13 28 / 14 29 / 15 30	13 28 / 14 29 / 15 30	VI				
				Final Score:							Official Verification	

Subs: 1 2 3 4 5 6 7 8 9 10 11 12 13 14 15 16 17 18   Subs: 1 2 3 4 5 6 7 8 9 10 11 12 13 14 15 16 17 18

Comments: ....   Comments: ....

Referee: ....   Umpire: ....

Scorekeeper: ....

Key: C=Playing Captain   1=Point   ⊣ =Loss of Rally   ☐ =Point Scored Off Loss of Rally   △ =Libero Point

P-1=Penalty Point   P=Penalty   Px=Penalty Opponent   R=Reply   Rs=Re-Serve

T= Time-out   TX=Time-out Opponent   S=Substitution Serving Team   Sx=Opponent Substitution

If the receiving team wins the rally, it receives a point which is recorded on the line of the NEXT server's
a number and a square is drawn around it. Also draw a square around the same point on the team's running score.

Date: **Home:** **Visitor:** **Set #:**

Time-Outs		Game No:			First Serve (Check Box Below)		Time-Outs			

Serve Order	Player No	Team:					L:									First Serve (Check Box Below)		Serve Order	Player No	Team:						L:								
I																1 16 / 2 17	1 16 / 2 17	I																
II																3 18 / 4 19 / 5 20	3 18 / 4 19 / 5 20	II																
III																6 21 / 7 22	6 21 / 7 22	III																
IV																8 23 / 9 24 / 10 25	8 23 / 9 24 / 10 25	IV																
V																11 26 / 12 27 / 13 28	11 26 / 12 27 / 13 28	V																
VI																14 29 / 15 30	14 29 / 15 30	VI																
										Final Score:															**Official Verification**								

Subs: 1 2 3 4 5 6 7 8 9 10 11 12 13 14 15 16 17 18   **Subs:** 1 2 3 4 5 6 7 8 9 10 11 12 13 14 15 16 17 18

Comments: ....   Comments: ....

Referee: ....   Umpire: ....

Scorekeeper: ....

Key:
C=Playing Captain   1=Point   ⊣ =Loss of Rally   ☐ =Point Scored Off Loss of Rally   △ =Libero Point
P-1=Penalty Point   P=Penalty   Px=Penalty Opponent   R=Reply   Rs=Re-Serve
T= Time-out   TX=Time-out Opponent   S=Substitution Serving Team   Sx=Opponent Substitution

If the receiving team wins the rally, it receives a point which is recorded on the line of the NEXT server's
a number and a square is drawn around it. Also draw a square around the same point on the team's running score.

Date: Home: Visitor: Set #:

Time-Outs		Game No:			First Serve (Check Box Below)		Time-Outs			

Serve Order	Player No	Team:	L:				Serve Order	Player No	Team:	L:
I				1 16	1 16		I			
				2 17	2 17					
II				3 18	3 18		II			
				4 19	4 19					
				5 20	5 20					
III				6 21	6 21		III			
				7 22	7 22					
				8 23	8 23					
IV				9 24	9 24		IV			
				10 25	10 25					
				11 26	11 26					
V				12 27	12 27		V			
				13 28	13 28					
				14 29	14 29					
VI				15 30	15 30		VI			

Final Score:			Official Verification	

Subs: 1 2 3 4 5 6 7 8 9 10 11 12 13 14 15 16 17 18   Subs: 1 2 3 4 5 6 7 8 9 10 11 12 13 14 15 16 17 18

Comments: ....

Comments: ....

Referee: ....   Umpire: ....

Scorekeeper: ....

Key:
C=Playing Captain   1=Point   ⊣ =Loss of Rally   ☐ =Point Scored Off Loss of Rally   △ =Libero Point
P-1=Penalty Point   P=Penalty   Px=Penalty Opponent   R=Reply   Rs=Re-Serve
T= Time-out   TX=Time-out Opponent   S=Substitution Serving Team   Sx=Opponent Substitution

If the receiving team wins the rally, it receives a point which is recorded on the line of the NEXT server's
a number and a square is drawn around it. Also draw a square around the same point on the team's running score.

Date: Home: Visitor: Set #:

Time-Outs		Game No:			First Serve (Check Box Below)		Time-Outs			
Serve Order	**Player No**	**Team:**	**L:**				**Serve Order**	**Player No**	**Team:**	**L:**
I					1 16 2 17	1 16 2 17	I			
II					3 18 4 19 5 20	3 18 4 19 5 20	II			
III					6 21 7 22	6 21 7 22	III			
IV					8 23 9 24 10 25	8 23 9 24 10 25	IV			
V					11 26 12 27 13 28	11 26 12 27 13 28	V			
VI					14 29 15 30	14 29 15 30	VI			
			Final Score:						**Official Verification**	

Subs: 1 2 3 4 5 6 7 8 9 10 11 12 13 14 15 16 17 18   Subs: 1 2 3 4 5 6 7 8 9 10 11 12 13 14 15 16 17 18

Comments: ....   Comments: ....

Referee: ....   Umpire: ....

Scorekeeper: ....

Key:
C=Playing Captain	1=Point	⊣ =Loss of Rally	☐ =Point Scored Off Loss of Rally	△ =Libero Point
P-1=Penalty Point	P=Penalty	Px=Penalty Opponent	R=Reply	Rs=Re-Serve
T= Time-out	TX=Time-out Opponent	S=Substitution Serving Team	Sx=Opponent Substitution	

If the receiving team wins the rally, it receives a point which is recorded on the line of the NEXT server's
a number and a square is drawn around it. Also draw a square around the same point on the team's running score.

| Date: | | Home: | | Visitor: | | Set #: |

| Time-Outs | | Game No: | | First Serve (Check Box Below) | | Time-Outs | | |

Serve Order	Player No	Team:	L:			Serve Order	Player No	Team:	L:
I				1 16	1 16	I			
				2 17	2 17				
II				3 18	3 18	II			
				4 19	4 19				
				5 20	5 20				
III				6 21	6 21	III			
				7 22	7 22				
				8 23	8 23				
IV				9 24	9 24	IV			
				10 25	10 25				
V				11 26	11 26	V			
				12 27	12 27				
				13 28	13 28				
VI				14 29	14 29	VI			
				15 30	15 30				
			Final Score:					Official Verification	

Subs: 1 2 3 4 5 6 7 8 9 10 11 12 13 14 15 16 17 18

Subs: 1 2 3 4 5 6 7 8 9 10 11 12 13 14 15 16 17 18

Comments: ....

Comments: ....

....

....

Referee: ....

Umpire: ....

Scorekeeper: ....

Key:

C=Playing Captain	1=Point	⊣ =Loss of Rally	☐ =Point Scored Off Loss of Rally	△ =Libero Point
P-1=Penalty Point	P=Penalty	Px=Penalty Opponent	R=Reply	Rs=Re-Serve
T= Time-out	TX=Time-out Opponent	S=Substitution Serving Team	Sx=Opponent Substitution	

If the receiving team wins the rally, it receives a point which is recorded on the line of the NEXT server's
a number and a square is drawn around it. Also draw a square around the same point on the team's running score.

Date: Home: Visitor: Set #:

Time-Outs		Game No:			First Serve (Check Box Below)		Time-Outs			

Serve Order	Player No	Team:				L:			Serve Order	Player No	Team:			L:

			First column numbers	Second column numbers	
I			1 16 / 2 17	1 16 / 2 17	I
II			3 18 / 4 19 / 5 20	3 18 / 4 19 / 5 20	II
III			6 21 / 7 22	6 21 / 7 22	III
IV			8 23 / 9 24 / 10 25	8 23 / 9 24 / 10 25	IV
V			11 26 / 12 27 / 13 28	11 26 / 12 27 / 13 28	V
VI			14 29 / 15 30	14 29 / 15 30	VI

Final Score: Official Verification

Subs: 1 2 3 4 5 6 7 8 9 10 11 12 13 14 15 16 17 18   Subs: 1 2 3 4 5 6 7 8 9 10 11 12 13 14 15 16 17 18

Comments: .... Comments: ....

Referee: .... Umpire: ....

Scorekeeper: ....

Key:

C=Playing Captain	1=Point	⊣ =Loss of Rally ☐ =Point Scored Off Loss of Rally △ =Libero Point
P-1=Penalty Point	P=Penalty	Px=Penalty Opponent R=Reply Rs=Re-Serve
T= Time-out	TX=Time-out Opponent	S=Substitution Serving Team Sx=Opponent Substitution

If the receiving team wins the rally, it receives a point which is recorded on the line of the NEXT server's
a number and a square is drawn around it. Also draw a square around the same point on the team's running score.

Date: Home: Visitor: Set #:

Time-Outs		Game No:				First Serve (Check Box Below)		Time-Outs			

| Serve Order | Player No | Team: | | | | | | L: | | | | | | | | Serve Order | Player No | Team: | | | | | | L: | | | | | |

Serve Order				Serve Order	
I		1 16 / 2 17	1 16 / 2 17	I	
II		3 18 / 4 19 / 5 20	3 18 / 4 19 / 5 20	II	
III		6 21 / 7 22	6 21 / 7 22	III	
IV		8 23 / 9 24 / 10 25	8 23 / 9 24 / 10 25	IV	
V		11 26 / 12 27 / 13 28	11 26 / 12 27 / 13 28	V	
VI		14 29 / 15 30	14 29 / 15 30	VI	

Final Score: | | Official Verification

Subs: 1 2 3 4 5 6 7 8 9 10 11 12 13 14 15 16 17 18   Subs: 1 2 3 4 5 6 7 8 9 10 11 12 13 14 15 16 17 18

Comments: ....   Comments: ....

Referee: ....   Umpire: ....

Scorekeeper: ....

Key:

C=Playing Captain	1=Point	⊣ =Loss of Rally	☐ =Point Scored Off Loss of Rally	△ =Libero Point
P-1=Penalty Point	P=Penalty	Px=Penalty Opponent	R=Reply	Rs=Re-Serve
T= Time-out	TX=Time-out Opponent	S=Substitution Serving Team	Sx=Opponent Substitution	

If the receiving team wins the rally, it receives a point which is recorded on the line of the NEXT server's
a number and a square is drawn around it. Also draw a square around the same point on the team's running score.

Date: Home: Visitor: Set #:

Time-Outs		Game No:		First Serve (Check Box Below)		Time-Outs		Team:		L:

| Serve Order | Player No | Team: L: | | | | Serve Order | Player No | Team: L: |

| Serve Order | Player No | Team: | | | | | | | | | | | | Serve Order | Player No | Team: | | | | | | | | | |

Left numbers column:
1 16
2 17
3 18
4 19
5 20
6 21
7 22
8 23
9 24
10 25
11 26
12 27
13 28
14 29
15 30

Right numbers column:
1 16
2 17
3 18
4 19
5 20
6 21
7 22
8 23
9 24
10 25
11 26
12 27
13 28
14 29
15 30

Serve Order (left): I, II, III, IV, V, VI
Serve Order (right): I, II, III, IV, V, VI

Final Score:

Official Verification

Subs: 1 2 3 4 5 6 7 8 9 10 11 12 13 14 15 16 17 18

Subs: 1 2 3 4 5 6 7 8 9 10 11 12 13 14 15 16 17 18

Comments: ....

Comments: ....

Referee: ....

Umpire: ....

Scorekeeper: ....

Key:

C=Playing Captain	1=Point	⊣ =Loss of Rally	☐ =Point Scored Off Loss of Rally	△ =Libero Point
P-1=Penalty Point	P=Penalty	Px=Penalty Opponent	R=Reply	Rs=Re-Serve
T= Time-out	TX=Time-out Opponent	S=Substitution Serving Team	Sx=Opponent Substitution	

If the receiving team wins the rally, it receives a point which is recorded on the line of the NEXT server's
a number and a square is drawn around it. Also draw a square around the same point on the team's running score.

Date: Home: Visitor: Set #:

Time-Outs		Game No:		First Serve (Check Box Below)		Time-Outs			

Serve Order	Player No	Team: L:			Serve Order	Player No	Team: L:
I			1 16 / 2 17	1 16 / 2 17	I		
II			3 18 / 4 19 / 5 20	3 18 / 4 19 / 5 20	II		
III			6 21 / 7 22	6 21 / 7 22	III		
IV			8 23 / 9 24 / 10 25	8 23 / 9 24 / 10 25	IV		
V			11 26 / 12 27 / 13 28	11 26 / 12 27 / 13 28	V		
VI			14 29 / 15 30	14 29 / 15 30	VI		
Final Score:					Official Verification		

Subs: 1 2 3 4 5 6 7 8 9 10 11 12 13 14 15 16 17 18   Subs: 1 2 3 4 5 6 7 8 9 10 11 12 13 14 15 16 17 18

Comments: ....   Comments: ....

Referee: ....   Umpire: ....

Scorekeeper: ....

Key:

C=Playing Captain	1=Point	⊣ =Loss of Rally	□ =Point Scored Off Loss of Rally	△ =Libero Point
P-1=Penalty Point	P=Penalty	Px=Penalty Opponent	R=Reply	Rs=Re-Serve
T= Time-out	TX=Time-out Opponent	S=Substitution Serving Team	Sx=Opponent Substitution	

If the receiving team wins the rally, it receives a point which is recorded on the line of the NEXT server's
a number and a square is drawn around it. Also draw a square around the same point on the team's running score.

Date: Home: Visitor: Set #:

Time-Outs		Game No:												First Serve (Check Box Below)		Time-Outs			

Serve Order	Player No	Team: L:															Serve Order	Player No	Team: L:

Serve Order	First Serve (Home)	First Serve (Visitor)	Serve Order
I	1 16 / 2 17	1 16 / 2 17	I
II	3 18 / 4 19 / 5 20	3 18 / 4 19 / 5 20	II
III	6 21 / 7 22	6 21 / 7 22	III
IV	8 23 / 9 24 / 10 25	8 23 / 9 24 / 10 25	IV
V	11 26 / 12 27 / 13 28	11 26 / 12 27 / 13 28	V
VI	14 29 / 15 30	14 29 / 15 30	VI

Final Score: Official Verification

Subs: 1 2 3 4 5 6 7 8 9 10 11 12 13 14 15 16 17 18   Subs: 1 2 3 4 5 6 7 8 9 10 11 12 13 14 15 16 17 18

Comments: ....   Comments: ....

Referee: ....   Umpire: ....

Scorekeeper: ....

Key: C=Playing Captain   1=Point   ⊣ =Loss of Rally   ☐ =Point Scored Off Loss of Rally   △ =Libero Point

      P-1=Penalty Point   P=Penalty   Px=Penalty Opponent   R=Reply   Rs=Re-Serve

      T= Time-out   TX=Time-out Opponent   S=Substitution Serving Team   Sx=Opponent Substitution

If the receiving team wins the rally, it receives a point which is recorded on the line of the NEXT server's
a number and a square is drawn around it. Also draw a square around the same point on the team's running score.

Date: Home: Visitor: Set #:

Time-Outs		Game No:					First Serve (Check Box Below)		Time-Outs			

Serve Order	Player No	Team:						L:								1 16	1 16	Serve Order	Player No	Team:								L:						
I																2 17 3 18 4 19	2 17 3 18 4 19	I															
II																5 20 6 21 7 22	5 20 6 21 7 22	II															
III																8 23 9 24 10 25	8 23 9 24 10 25	III															
IV																11 26 12 27 13 28	11 26 12 27 13 28	IV															
V																14 29 15 30	14 29 15 30	V															
VI																		VI															
										Final Score:																Official Verification						

Subs: 1 2 3 4 5 6 7 8 9 10 11 12 13 14 15 16 17 18   Subs: 1 2 3 4 5 6 7 8 9 10 11 12 13 14 15 16 17 18

Comments: ....   Comments: ....

Referee: ....   Umpire: ....

Scorekeeper: ....

Key:

C=Playing Captain	1=Point	⊣ =Loss of Rally	☐ =Point Scored Off Loss of Rally	△ =Libero Point
P-1=Penalty Point	P=Penalty	Px=Penalty Opponent	R=Reply	Rs=Re-Serve
T= Time-out	TX=Time-out Opponent	S=Substitution Serving Team	Sx=Opponent Substitution	

If the receiving team wins the rally, it receives a point which is recorded on the line of the NEXT server's
a number and a square is drawn around it. Also draw a square around the same point on the team's running score.

Date:	Home:	Visitor:	Set #:

Time-Outs		Game No:		First Serve (Check Box Below)		Time-Outs		

Serve Order	Player No	Team:											L:						Serve Order	Player No	Team:										L:				

Serve Order	...		First Serve col 1	First Serve col 2	Serve Order	...
I			1 16 / 2 17	1 16 / 2 17	I	
II			3 18 / 4 19 / 5 20	3 18 / 4 19 / 5 20	II	
III			6 21 / 7 22 / 8 23	6 21 / 7 22 / 8 23	III	
IV			9 24 / 10 25	9 24 / 10 25	IV	
V			11 26 / 12 27 / 13 28	11 26 / 12 27 / 13 28	V	
VI			14 29 / 15 30	14 29 / 15 30	VI	

Final Score:		Official Verification	

Subs: 1 2 3 4 5 6 7 8 9 10 11 12 13 14 15 16 17 18   Subs: 1 2 3 4 5 6 7 8 9 10 11 12 13 14 15 16 17 18

Comments: ....   Comments: ....

Referee: ....   Umpire: ....

Scorekeeper: ....

Key:

C=Playing Captain	1=Point	⊣ =Loss of Rally	☐ =Point Scored Off Loss of Rally	△ =Libero Point
P-1=Penalty Point	P=Penalty	Px=Penalty Opponent	R=Reply	Rs=Re-Serve
T= Time-out	TX=Time-out Opponent	S=Substitution Serving Team	Sx=Opponent Substitution	

If the receiving team wins the rally, it receives a point which is recorded on the line of the NEXT server's
a number and a square is drawn around it. Also draw a square around the same point on the team's running score.

Date: Home: Visitor: Set #:

| Time-Outs | | Game No: | | | First Serve (Check Box Below) | | Time-Outs | | | |

| Serve Order | Player No | Team: | | | | | | L: | | | | | | | | | | Serve Order | Player No | Team: | | | | | | L: | | | | | | |

I									1 16	1 16	I								
									2 17	2 17									
II									3 18	3 18	II								
									4 19	4 19									
									5 20	5 20									
III									6 21	6 21	III								
									7 22	7 22									
IV									8 23	8 23	IV								
									9 24	9 24									
									10 25	10 25									
V									11 26	11 26	V								
									12 27	12 27									
									13 28	13 28									
VI									14 29	14 29	VI								
									15 30	15 30									

Final Score: Official Verification

Subs: **1 2 3 4 5 6 7 8 9 10 11 12 13 14 15 16 17 18**   Subs: **1 2 3 4 5 6 7 8 9 10 11 12 13 14 15 16 17 18**

Comments: ....   Comments: ....

Referee: ....   Umpire: ....

Scorekeeper: ....

Key:

C=Playing Captain	1=Point	⊣ =Loss of Rally	☐ =Point Scored Off Loss of Rally	△ =Libero Point
P-1=Penalty Point	P=Penalty	Px=Penalty Opponent	R=Reply	Rs=Re-Serve
T= Time-out	TX=Time-out Opponent	S=Substitution Serving Team	Sx=Opponent Substitution	

If the receiving team wins the rally, it receives a point which is recorded on the line of the NEXT server's
a number and a square is drawn around it. Also draw a square around the same point on the team's running score.

Date: Home: Visitor: Set #:

Time-Outs		Game No:		First Serve (Check Box Below)		Time-Outs			

Serve Order	Player No	Team:	L:			Serve Order	Player No	Team:	L:
I				1 16 / 2 17	1 16 / 2 17	I			
II				3 18 / 4 19 / 5 20	3 18 / 4 19 / 5 20	II			
III				6 21 / 7 22	6 21 / 7 22	III			
IV				8 23 / 9 24 / 10 25	8 23 / 9 24 / 10 25	IV			
V				11 26 / 12 27 / 13 28	11 26 / 12 27 / 13 28	V			
VI				14 29 / 15 30	14 29 / 15 30	VI			

Final Score: Official Verification

Subs: 1 2 3 4 5 6 7 8 9 10 11 12 13 14 15 16 17 18   Subs: 1 2 3 4 5 6 7 8 9 10 11 12 13 14 15 16 17 18

Comments: ....   Comments: ....

Referee: ....   Umpire: ....

Scorekeeper: ....

Key: C=Playing Captain   1=Point   ⊣ =Loss of Rally   ☐ =Point Scored Off Loss of Rally   △ =Libero Point

P-1=Penalty Point   P=Penalty   Px=Penalty Opponent   R=Reply   Rs=Re-Serve

T= Time-out   TX=Time-out Opponent   S=Substitution Serving Team   Sx=Opponent Substitution

If the receiving team wins the rally, it receives a point which is recorded on the line of the NEXT server's
a number and a square is drawn around it. Also draw a square around the same point on the team's running score.

Date: Home: Visitor: Set #:

Time-Outs		Game No:			First Serve (Check Box Below)		Time-Outs			
Serve Order	Player No	Team:	L:				Serve Order	Player No	Team:	L:
I					1 16 / 2 17	1 16 / 2 17	I			
II					3 18 / 4 19 / 5 20	3 18 / 4 19 / 5 20	II			
III					6 21 / 7 22 / 8 23	6 21 / 7 22 / 8 23	III			
IV					9 24 / 10 25	9 24 / 10 25	IV			
V					11 26 / 12 27 / 13 28	11 26 / 12 27 / 13 28	V			
VI					14 29 / 15 30	14 29 / 15 30	VI			
			Final Score:						Official Verification	

Subs: 1 2 3 4 5 6 7 8 9 10 11 12 13 14 15 16 17 18   Subs: 1 2 3 4 5 6 7 8 9 10 11 12 13 14 15 16 17 18

Comments: ....   Comments: ....

Referee: ....   Umpire: ....

Scorekeeper: ....

Key:

C=Playing Captain	1=Point	⊣ =Loss of Rally	☐ =Point Scored Off Loss of Rally	△ =Libero Point
P-1=Penalty Point	P=Penalty	Px=Penalty Opponent	R=Reply	Rs=Re-Serve
T= Time-out	TX=Time-out Opponent	S=Substitution Serving Team	Sx=Opponent Substitution	

If the receiving team wins the rally, it receives a point which is recorded on the line of the NEXT server's
a number and a square is drawn around it. Also draw a square around the same point on the team's running score.

Date: Home: Visitor: Set #:

Time-Outs		Game No:			First Serve (Check Box Below)		Time-Outs			
Serve Order	Player No	**Team:**		**L:**			Serve Order	Player No	**Team:**	**L:**
I					1 16 2 17	1 16 2 17	I			
II					3 18 4 19 5 20	3 18 4 19 5 20	II			
III					6 21 7 22	6 21 7 22	III			
IV					8 23 9 24 10 25	8 23 9 24 10 25	IV			
V					11 26 12 27 13 28	11 26 12 27 13 28	V			
VI					14 29 15 30	14 29 15 30	VI			
			Final Score:						**Official Verification**	

Subs: 1 2 3 4 5 6 7 8 9 10 11 12 13 14 15 16 17 18   Subs: 1 2 3 4 5 6 7 8 9 10 11 12 13 14 15 16 17 18

Comments: ....   Comments: ....

Referee: ....   Umpire: ....

Scorekeeper: ....

Key:

C=Playing Captain	1=Point	⊣ =Loss of Rally	☐ =Point Scored Off Loss of Rally	△ =Libero Point
P-1=Penalty Point	P=Penalty	Px=Penalty Opponent	R=Reply	Rs=Re-Serve
T= Time-out	TX=Time-out Opponent	S=Substitution Serving Team	Sx=Opponent Substitution	

If the receiving team wins the rally, it receives a point which is recorded on the line of the NEXT server's
a number and a square is drawn around it. Also draw a square around the same point on the team's running score.

Date: _____ Home: _____ Visitor: _____ Set #: _____

Time-Outs		Game No:					First Serve (Check Box Below)		Time-Outs			

Serve Order	Player No	Team:				L:				Serve Order	Player No	Team:				L:

I								1 16	1 16	I						
								2 17	2 17							
II								3 18	3 18	II						
								4 19	4 19							
								5 20	5 20							
III								6 21	6 21	III						
								7 22	7 22							
								8 23	8 23							
IV								9 24	9 24	IV						
								10 25	10 25							
V								11 26	11 26	V						
								12 27	12 27							
								13 28	13 28							
VI								14 29	14 29	VI						
								15 30	15 30							

Final Score: _____ Official Verification: _____

Subs: 1 2 3 4 5 6 7 8 9 10 11 12 13 14 15 16 17 18   Subs: 1 2 3 4 5 6 7 8 9 10 11 12 13 14 15 16 17 18

Comments: ....   Comments: ....

Referee: ....   Umpire: ....

Scorekeeper: ....

Key:

C=Playing Captain	1=Point	⊣ =Loss of Rally	☐ =Point Scored Off Loss of Rally	△ =Libero Point
P-1=Penalty Point	P=Penalty	Px=Penalty Opponent	R=Reply	Rs=Re-Serve
T= Time-out	TX=Time-out Opponent	S=Substitution Serving Team	Sx=Opponent Substitution	

If the receiving team wins the rally, it receives a point which is recorded on the line of the NEXT server's
a number and a square is drawn around it. Also draw a square around the same point on the team's running score.

Date: Home: Visitor: Set #:

Time-Outs		Game No:			First Serve (Check Box Below)		Time-Outs			

Serve Order	Player No	Team:				L:			Serve Order	Player No	Team:		L:

I								1 16	1 16	I			
II								2 17 3 18	2 17 3 18	II			
								4 19	4 19				
								5 20	5 20				
III								6 21	6 21	III			
								7 22	7 22				
								8 23	8 23				
IV								9 24	9 24	IV			
								10 25	10 25				
V								11 26	11 26	V			
								12 27	12 27				
								13 28	13 28				
VI								14 29	14 29	VI			
								15 30	15 30				

Final Score: Official Verification

Subs: 1 2 3 4 5 6 7 8 9 10 11 12 13 14 15 16 17 18   Subs: 1 2 3 4 5 6 7 8 9 10 11 12 13 14 15 16 17 18

Comments: ....   Comments: ....

Referee: ....   Umpire: ....

Scorekeeper: ....

Key:
C=Playing Captain	1=Point	⊣ =Loss of Rally	☐ =Point Scored Off Loss of Rally	△ =Libero Point
P-1=Penalty Point	P=Penalty	Px=Penalty Opponent	R=Reply	Rs=Re-Serve
T= Time-out	TX=Time-out Opponent	S=Substitution Serving Team	Sx=Opponent Substitution	

If the receiving team wins the rally, it receives a point which is recorded on the line of the NEXT server's
a number and a square is drawn around it. Also draw a square around the same point on the team's running score.

Date: Home: Visitor: Set #:

Time-Outs		Game No:					First Serve (Check Box Below)		Time-Outs		Team:		L:			

Serve Order	Player No	Team:					L:													Serve Order	Player No	Team:					L:					
I															1 16 / 2 17	1 16 / 2 17	I											
II															3 18 / 4 19 / 5 20	3 18 / 4 19 / 5 20	II											
III															6 21 / 7 22	6 21 / 7 22	III											
IV															8 23 / 9 24 / 10 25	8 23 / 9 24 / 10 25	IV											
V															11 26 / 12 27 / 13 28	11 26 / 12 27 / 13 28	V											
VI															14 29 / 15 30	14 29 / 15 30	VI											

Final Score: Official Verification

Subs: 1 2 3 4 5 6 7 8 9 10 11 12 13 14 15 16 17 18   Subs: 1 2 3 4 5 6 7 8 9 10 11 12 13 14 15 16 17 18

Comments: ....   Comments: ....

Referee: ....   Umpire: ....

Scorekeeper: ....

Key: C=Playing Captain   1=Point   ⊣ =Loss of Rally   ☐ =Point Scored Off Loss of Rally   △ =Libero Point
P-1=Penalty Point   P=Penalty   Px=Penalty Opponent   R=Reply   Rs=Re-Serve
T= Time-out   TX=Time-out Opponent   S=Substitution Serving Team   Sx=Opponent Substitution

If the receiving team wins the rally, it receives a point which is recorded on the line of the NEXT server's
a number and a square is drawn around it. Also draw a square around the same point on the team's running score.

Date: Home: Visitor: Set #:

Time-Outs		Game No:			First Serve (Check Box Below)		Time-Outs		Team:	L:

<table>
<tr><td colspan="2">Time-Outs</td><td rowspan="2">Game No:</td><td></td><td></td><td colspan="2">First Serve
(Check Box Below)</td><td colspan="2">Time-Outs</td><td></td><td></td></tr>
<tr><td></td><td></td><td></td><td></td><td></td><td></td><td></td><td></td><td></td><td></td></tr>
<tr><td>Serve Order</td><td>Player No</td><td colspan="2">Team:</td><td>L:</td><td></td><td></td><td>Serve Order</td><td>Player No</td><td colspan="2">Team:</td><td>L:</td></tr>
<tr><td>I</td><td></td><td colspan="3"></td><td>1 16
2 17</td><td>1 16
2 17</td><td>I</td><td></td><td colspan="3"></td></tr>
<tr><td>II</td><td></td><td colspan="3"></td><td>3 18
4 19
5 20</td><td>3 18
4 19
5 20</td><td>II</td><td></td><td colspan="3"></td></tr>
<tr><td>III</td><td></td><td colspan="3"></td><td>6 21
7 22
8 23</td><td>6 21
7 22
8 23</td><td>III</td><td></td><td colspan="3"></td></tr>
<tr><td>IV</td><td></td><td colspan="3"></td><td>9 24
10 25</td><td>9 24
10 25</td><td>IV</td><td></td><td colspan="3"></td></tr>
<tr><td>V</td><td></td><td colspan="3"></td><td>11 26
12 27
13 28</td><td>11 26
12 27
13 28</td><td>V</td><td></td><td colspan="3"></td></tr>
<tr><td>VI</td><td></td><td colspan="3"></td><td>14 29
15 30</td><td>14 29
15 30</td><td>VI</td><td></td><td colspan="3"></td></tr>
<tr><td colspan="5">Final Score:</td><td></td><td></td><td colspan="5">Official Verification</td></tr>
</table>

Subs: 1 2 3 4 5 6 7 8 9 10 11 12 13 14 15 16 17 18   Subs: 1 2 3 4 5 6 7 8 9 10 11 12 13 14 15 16 17 18

Comments: ....   Comments: ....
....

Referee: ....   Umpire: ....

Scorekeeper: ....

Key:

C=Playing Captain	1=Point	⊣ =Loss of Rally	☐ =Point Scored Off Loss of Rally	△ =Libero Point
P-1=Penalty Point	P=Penalty	Px=Penalty Opponent	R=Reply	Rs=Re-Serve
T= Time-out	TX=Time-out Opponent	S=Substitution Serving Team	Sx=Opponent Substitution	

If the receiving team wins the rally, it receives a point which is recorded on the line of the NEXT server's
a number and a square is drawn around it. Also draw a square around the same point on the team's running score.

| Date: | Home: | Visitor: | Set #: |

Time-Outs		Game No:	First Serve (Check Box Below)		Time-Outs		

Serve Order	Player No	Team:				L:					1 16 2 17	1 16 2 17	Serve Order	Player No	Team:					L:				
I											3 18 4 19 5 20	3 18 4 19 5 20	I											
II											6 21 7 22	6 21 7 22	II											
III											8 23 9 24 10 25	8 23 9 24 10 25	III											
IV											11 26 12 27 13 28	11 26 12 27 13 28	IV											
V											14 29 15 30	14 29 15 30	V											
VI													VI											
								Final Score:											Official Verification					

Subs: 1 2 3 4 5 6 7 8 9 10 11 12 13 14 15 16 17 18   Subs: 1 2 3 4 5 6 7 8 9 10 11 12 13 14 15 16 17 18

Comments: ....   Comments: ....

Referee: ....   Umpire: ....

Scorekeeper: ....

Key:

C=Playing Captain	1=Point	⊣ =Loss of Rally	☐ =Point Scored Off Loss of Rally	△ =Libero Point
P-1=Penalty Point	P=Penalty	Px=Penalty Opponent	R=Reply	Rs=Re-Serve
T= Time-out	TX=Time-out Opponent	S=Substitution Serving Team	Sx=Opponent Substitution	

If the receiving team wins the rally, it receives a point which is recorded on the line of the NEXT server's
a number and a square is drawn around it. Also draw a square around the same point on the team's running score.

Date: Home: Visitor: Set #:

Time-Outs		Game No:			First Serve (Check Box Below)		Time-Outs			
Serve Order	Player No	Team:	L:				Serve Order	Player No	Team:	L:
I					1 16 2 17	1 16 2 17	I			
II					3 18 4 19 5 20	3 18 4 19 5 20	II			
III					6 21 7 22	6 21 7 22	III			
IV					8 23 9 24 10 25	8 23 9 24 10 25	IV			
V					11 26 12 27 13 28	11 26 12 27 13 28	V			
VI					14 29 15 30	14 29 15 30	VI			
			Final Score:						Official Verification	

Subs: 1 2 3 4 5 6 7 8 9 10 11 12 13 14 15 16 17 18   Subs: 1 2 3 4 5 6 7 8 9 10 11 12 13 14 15 16 17 18

Comments: ....   Comments: ....

Referee: ....   Umpire: ....

Scorekeeper: ....

Key:

C=Playing Captain	1=Point	⊣ =Loss of Rally	☐ =Point Scored Off Loss of Rally	△ =Libero Point
P-1=Penalty Point	P=Penalty	Px=Penalty Opponent	R=Reply	Rs=Re-Serve
T= Time-out	TX=Time-out Opponent	S=Substitution Serving Team	Sx=Opponent Substitution	

If the receiving team wins the rally, it receives a point which is recorded on the line of the NEXT server's
a number and a square is drawn around it. Also draw a square around the same point on the team's running score.

Date: Home: Visitor: Set #:

	Time-Outs					First Serve (Check Box Below)		Time-Outs			

Game No:

Serve Order	Player No	Team:	L:			Serve Order	Player No	Team:	L:

Serve Order (left)					1 16 / 2 17		Serve Order (right)			
I					1 16 1 16		I			
					2 17 2 17					
II					3 18 3 18		II			
					4 19 4 19					
					5 20 5 20					
III					6 21 6 21		III			
					7 22 7 22					
					8 23 8 23					
IV					9 24 9 24		IV			
					10 25 10 25					
V					11 26 11 26		V			
					12 27 12 27					
					13 28 13 28					
VI					14 29 14 29		VI			
					15 30 15 30					

Final Score: **Official Verification**

Subs: 1 2 3 4 5 6 7 8 9 10 11 12 13 14 15 16 17 18   Subs: 1 2 3 4 5 6 7 8 9 10 11 12 13 14 15 16 17 18

Comments: ....   Comments: ....

Referee: ....   Umpire: ....

Scorekeeper: ....

Key:

C=Playing Captain	1=Point	⊣ =Loss of Rally	☐ =Point Scored Off Loss of Rally	△ =Libero Point
P-1=Penalty Point	P=Penalty	Px=Penalty Opponent	R=Reply	Rs=Re-Serve
T= Time-out	TX=Time-out Opponent	S=Substitution Serving Team	Sx=Opponent Substitution	

If the receiving team wins the rally, it receives a point which is recorded on the line of the NEXT server's
a number and a square is drawn around it. Also draw a square around the same point on the team's running score.

Date: Home: Visitor: Set #:

Time-Outs		Game No:	First Serve (Check Box Below)		Time-Outs		
Serve Order	Player No	Team: L:			Serve Order	Player No	Team: L:
I			1 16 2 17 3 18 4 19 5 20 6 21 7 22 8 23 9 24 10 25 11 26 12 27 13 28 14 29 15 30	1 16 2 17 3 18 4 19 5 20 6 21 7 22 8 23 9 24 10 25 11 26 12 27 13 28 14 29 15 30	I		
II					II		
III					III		
IV					IV		
V					V		
VI					VI		
		Final Score:				Official Verification	

Subs: 1 2 3 4 5 6 7 8 9 10 11 12 13 14 15 16 17 18

Subs: 1 2 3 4 5 6 7 8 9 10 11 12 13 14 15 16 17 18

Comments: ....

Comments: ....

Referee: ....

Umpire: ....

Scorekeeper: ....

Key:

C=Playing Captain	1=Point	⊣ =Loss of Rally	☐ =Point Scored Off Loss of Rally	△ =Libero Point
P-1=Penalty Point	P=Penalty	Px=Penalty Opponent	R=Reply	Rs=Re-Serve
T= Time-out	TX=Time-out Opponent	S=Substitution Serving Team	Sx=Opponent Substitution	

If the receiving team wins the rally, it receives a point which is recorded on the line of the NEXT server's a number and a square is drawn around it. Also draw a square around the same point on the team's running score.

Date: Home: Visitor: Set #:

Time-Outs		Game No:				First Serve (Check Box Below)		Time-Outs		Team:		L:

Serve Order	Player No	Team: L:							Serve Order	Player No	Team: L:
I			1 16	1 16	I		
II			2 17 3 18	2 17 3 18	II		
III			4 19 5 20 6 21 7 22	4 19 5 20 6 21 7 22	III		
IV			8 23 9 24 10 25	8 23 9 24 10 25	IV		
V			11 26 12 27 13 28	11 26 12 27 13 28	V		
VI			14 29 15 30	14 29 15 30	VI		

Final Score: Official Verification

Subs: 1 2 3 4 5 6 7 8 9 10 11 12 13 14 15 16 17 18   Subs: 1 2 3 4 5 6 7 8 9 10 11 12 13 14 15 16 17 18

Comments: ....   Comments: ....

Referee: ....   Umpire: ....

Scorekeeper: ....

Key:

C=Playing Captain	1=Point	⊣ =Loss of Rally	☐ =Point Scored Off Loss of Rally	△ =Libero Point
P-1=Penalty Point	P=Penalty	Px=Penalty Opponent	R=Reply	Rs=Re-Serve
T= Time-out	TX=Time-out Opponent	S=Substitution Serving Team	Sx=Opponent Substitution	

If the receiving team wins the rally, it receives a point which is recorded on the line of the NEXT server's
a number and a square is drawn around it. Also draw a square around the same point on the team's running score.

Date: Home: Visitor: Set #:

	Time-Outs	Game No:			First Serve (Check Box Below)		Time-Outs			

Serve Order	Player No	Team:	L:				Serve Order	Player No	Team:	L:
I					1 16	1 16	I			
					2 17	2 17				
II					3 18	3 18	II			
					4 19	4 19				
					5 20	5 20				
III					6 21	6 21	III			
					7 22	7 22				
					8 23	8 23				
IV					9 24	9 24	IV			
					10 25	10 25				
V					11 26	11 26	V			
					12 27	12 27				
					13 28	13 28				
VI					14 29	14 29	VI			
					15 30	15 30				
			Final Score:						Official Verification	

Subs: 1 2 3 4 5 6 7 8 9 10 11 12 13 14 15 16 17 18   Subs: 1 2 3 4 5 6 7 8 9 10 11 12 13 14 15 16 17 18

Comments: ....   Comments: ....

Referee: ....   Umpire: ....

Scorekeeper: ....

Key:
C=Playing Captain	1=Point	⊣ =Loss of Rally	☐ =Point Scored Off Loss of Rally	△ =Libero Point
P-1=Penalty Point	P=Penalty	Px=Penalty Opponent	R=Reply	Rs=Re-Serve
T= Time-out	TX=Time-out Opponent	S=Substitution Serving Team	Sx=Opponent Substitution	

If the receiving team wins the rally, it receives a point which is recorded on the line of the NEXT server's
a number and a square is drawn around it. Also draw a square around the same point on the team's running score.

Date: Home: Visitor: Set #:

	Time-Outs		Game No:					First Serve (Check Box Below)		Time-Outs			
Serve Order	Player No	Team:			L:					Serve Order	Player No	Team:	L:
I								1 16	1 16	I			
								2 17	2 17				
II								3 18	3 18	II			
								4 19	4 19				
								5 20	5 20				
III								6 21	6 21	III			
								7 22	7 22				
								8 23	8 23				
IV								9 24	9 24	IV			
								10 25	10 25				
V								11 26	11 26	V			
								12 27	12 27				
								13 28	13 28				
VI								14 29	14 29	VI			
								15 30	15 30				
				Final Score:								Official Verification	

Subs: 1 2 3 4 5 6 7 8 9 10 11 12 13 14 15 16 17 18   Subs: 1 2 3 4 5 6 7 8 9 10 11 12 13 14 15 16 17 18

Comments: ....   Comments: ....

Referee: ....   Umpire: ....

Scorekeeper: ....

Key: C=Playing Captain   1=Point   ⊣ =Loss of Rally   ☐ =Point Scored Off Loss of Rally   △ =Libero Point

P-1=Penalty Point   P=Penalty   Px=Penalty Opponent   R=Reply   Rs=Re-Serve

T= Time-out   TX=Time-out Opponent   S=Substitution Serving Team   Sx=Opponent Substitution

If the receiving team wins the rally, it receives a point which is recorded on the line of the NEXT server's
a number and a square is drawn around it. Also draw a square around the same point on the team's running score.

Date: Home: Visitor: Set #:

Time-Outs		Game No:			First Serve (Check Box Below)		Time-Outs			

Serve Order	Player No	Team:					L:				Serve Order	Player No	Team:		L:

I										1 16	1 16	I			
										2 17	2 17				
II										3 18	3 18	II			
										4 19	4 19				
										5 20	5 20				
III										6 21	6 21	III			
										7 22	7 22				
										8 23	8 23				
IV										9 24	9 24	IV			
										10 25	10 25				
V										11 26	11 26	V			
										12 27	12 27				
										13 28	13 28				
VI										14 29	14 29	VI			
										15 30	15 30				

Final Score: | | | Official Verification

Subs: 1 2 3 4 5 6 7 8 9 10 11 12 13 14 15 16 17 18   Subs: 1 2 3 4 5 6 7 8 9 10 11 12 13 14 15 16 17 18

Comments: ....   Comments: ....

Referee: ....   Umpire: ....

Scorekeeper: ....

Key:
C=Playing Captain	1=Point	⊣ =Loss of Rally	☐ =Point Scored Off Loss of Rally	△ =Libero Point
P-1=Penalty Point	P=Penalty	Px=Penalty Opponent	R=Reply	Rs=Re-Serve
T= Time-out	TX=Time-out Opponent	S=Substitution Serving Team	Sx=Opponent Substitution	

If the receiving team wins the rally, it receives a point which is recorded on the line of the NEXT server's
a number and a square is drawn around it. Also draw a square around the same point on the team's running score.

Date: Home: Visitor: Set #:

Time-Outs		Game No:				First Serve (Check Box Below)		Time-Outs			

Serve Order	Player No	Team:										L:					First Serve		Serve Order	Player No	Team:										L:	
I																	1 16 2 17	1 16 2 17	I													
II																	3 18 4 19 5 20	3 18 4 19 5 20	II													
III																	6 21 7 22	6 21 7 22	III													
IV																	8 23 9 24 10 25	8 23 9 24 10 25	IV													
V																	11 26 12 27 13 28	11 26 12 27 13 28	V													
VI																	14 29 15 30	14 29 15 30	VI													
												Final Score:																Official Verification				

Subs: 1 2 3 4 5 6 7 8 9 10 11 12 13 14 15 16 17 18   Subs: 1 2 3 4 5 6 7 8 9 10 11 12 13 14 15 16 17 18

Comments: ....   Comments: ....

Referee: ....   Umpire: ....

Scorekeeper: ....

Key:

C=Playing Captain	1=Point	⊣ =Loss of Rally	☐ =Point Scored Off Loss of Rally	△ =Libero Point
P-1=Penalty Point	P=Penalty	Px=Penalty Opponent	R=Reply	Rs=Re-Serve
T= Time-out	TX=Time-out Opponent	S=Substitution Serving Team	Sx=Opponent Substitution	

If the receiving team wins the rally, it receives a point which is recorded on the line of the NEXT server's
a number and a square is drawn around it. Also draw a square around the same point on the team's running score.

Date: Home: Visitor: Set #:

Time-Outs		Game No:			First Serve (Check Box Below)		Time-Outs			

Serve Order	Player No	Team:				L:			Serve Order	Player No	Team:			L:

I							1 16 / 2 17	1 16 / 2 17	I					
II							3 18 / 4 19 / 5 20	3 18 / 4 19 / 5 20	II					
III							6 21 / 7 22 / 8 23	6 21 / 7 22 / 8 23	III					
IV							9 24 / 10 25	9 24 / 10 25	IV					
V							11 26 / 12 27 / 13 28	11 26 / 12 27 / 13 28	V					
VI							14 29 / 15 30	14 29 / 15 30	VI					

Final Score: Official Verification

Subs: 1 2 3 4 5 6 7 8 9 10 11 12 13 14 15 16 17 18   Subs: 1 2 3 4 5 6 7 8 9 10 11 12 13 14 15 16 17 18

Comments: Comments:

Referee: Umpire:

Scorekeeper:

Key:

C=Playing Captain	1=Point	⊣ =Loss of Rally	☐ =Point Scored Off Loss of Rally	△ =Libero Point
P-1=Penalty Point	P=Penalty	Px=Penalty Opponent	R=Reply	Rs=Re-Serve
T= Time-out	TX=Time-out Opponent	S=Substitution Serving Team	Sx=Opponent Substitution	

If the receiving team wins the rally, it receives a point which is recorded on the line of the NEXT server's
a number and a square is drawn around it. Also draw a square around the same point on the team's running score.

Date:	Home:	Visitor:	Set #:

Time-Outs		Game No:		First Serve (Check Box Below)		Time-Outs			

Serve Order	Player No	Team:												L:							Serve Order	Player No	Team:											L:			
I																					1 16 / 2 17		I															
II																					3 18 / 4 19 / 5 20		II															
III																					6 21 / 7 22 / 8 23		III															
IV																					9 24 / 10 25		IV															
V																					11 26 / 12 27 / 13 28		V															
VI																					14 29 / 15 30		VI															

First Serve check box column listing: 1 16, 2 17, 3 18, 4 19, 5 20, 6 21, 7 22, 8 23, 9 24, 10 25, 11 26, 12 27, 13 28, 14 29, 15 30 (two columns)

Final Score: ___   Official Verification

Subs: 1 2 3 4 5 6 7 8 9 10 11 12 13 14 15 16 17 18   Subs: 1 2 3 4 5 6 7 8 9 10 11 12 13 14 15 16 17 18

Comments: ....   Comments: ....

Referee: ....   Umpire: ....

Scorekeeper: ....

Key:

C=Playing Captain	1=Point	⊣ =Loss of Rally	☐ =Point Scored Off Loss of Rally	△ =Libero Point
P-1=Penalty Point	P=Penalty	Px=Penalty Opponent	R=Reply	Rs=Re-Serve
T= Time-out	TX=Time-out Opponent	S=Substitution Serving Team	Sx=Opponent Substitution	

If the receiving team wins the rally, it receives a point which is recorded on the line of the NEXT server's
a number and a square is drawn around it. Also draw a square around the same point on the team's running score.

Date: Home: Visitor: Set #:

Time-Outs		Game No:		First Serve (Check Box Below)		Time-Outs			
Serve Order	Player No	Team:	L:			Serve Order	Player No	Team:	L:
I				1 16	1 16	I			
				2 17	2 17				
II				3 18	3 18	II			
				4 19	4 19				
				5 20	5 20				
III				6 21	6 21	III			
				7 22	7 22				
IV				8 23	8 23	IV			
				9 24	9 24				
				10 25	10 25				
V				11 26	11 26	V			
				12 27	12 27				
				13 28	13 28				
VI				14 29	14 29	VI			
				15 30	15 30				
			Final Score:					Official Verification	

Subs: 1 2 3 4 5 6 7 8 9 10 11 12 13 14 15 16 17 18   Subs: 1 2 3 4 5 6 7 8 9 10 11 12 13 14 15 16 17 18

Comments: ....   Comments: ....
....

Referee: ....   Umpire: ....

Scorekeeper: ....

Key: C=Playing Captain   1=Point   ⊣ =Loss of Rally   ☐ =Point Scored Off Loss of Rally   △ =Libero Point

P-1=Penalty Point   P=Penalty   Px=Penalty Opponent   R=Reply   Rs=Re-Serve

T= Time-out   TX=Time-out Opponent   S=Substitution Serving Team   Sx=Opponent Substitution

If the receiving team wins the rally, it receives a point which is recorded on the line of the NEXT server's
a number and a square is drawn around it. Also draw a square around the same point on the team's running score.

Date: Home: Visitor: Set #:

Time-Outs		Game No:	First Serve (Check Box Below)		Time-Outs		

Serve Order	Player No	Team: L:			Serve Order	Player No	Team: L:
I					I		
II					II		
III					III		
IV					IV		
V					V		
VI					VI		
		Final Score:			Official Verification		

First Serve			
1	16	1	16
2	17	2	17
3	18	3	18
4	19	4	19
5	20	5	20
6	21	6	21
7	22	7	22
8	23	8	23
9	24	9	24
10	25	10	25
11	26	11	26
12	27	12	27
13	28	13	28
14	29	14	29
15	30	15	30

Subs: **1 2 3 4 5 6 7 8 9 10 11 12 13 14 15 16 17 18**

Subs: **1 2 3 4 5 6 7 8 9 10 11 12 13 14 15 16 17 18**

Comments: ....

Comments: ....

Referee: ....

Umpire: ....

Scorekeeper: ....

Key:

C=Playing Captain	**1=Point**	**⊣ =Loss of Rally**	**☐ =Point Scored Off Loss of Rally**	**△ =Libero Point**
P-1=Penalty Point	**P=Penalty**	**Px=Penalty Opponent**	**R=Reply**	**Rs=Re-Serve**
T= Time-out	**TX=Time-out Opponent**	**S=Substitution Serving Team**	**Sx=Opponent Substitution**	

If the receiving team wins the rally, it receives a point which is recorded on the line of the NEXT server's a number and a square is drawn around it. Also draw a square around the same point on the team's running score.

Date: _____ Home: _____ Visitor: _____ Set #: _____

	Time-Outs		Game No:				First Serve (Check Box Below)			Time-Outs			
Serve Order	Player No	Team:		L:					Serve Order	Player No	Team:		L:
I						1 16	1 16		I				
						2 17	2 17						
II						3 18	3 18		II				
						4 19	4 19						
						5 20	5 20						
III						6 21	6 21		III				
						7 22	7 22						
						8 23	8 23						
IV						9 24	9 24		IV				
						10 25	10 25						
V						11 26	11 26		V				
						12 27	12 27						
						13 28	13 28						
VI						14 29	14 29		VI				
						15 30	15 30						
				Final Score:								Official Verification	

Subs: 1 2 3 4 5 6 7 8 9 10 11 12 13 14 15 16 17 18   Subs: 1 2 3 4 5 6 7 8 9 10 11 12 13 14 15 16 17 18

Comments: ....   Comments: ....

Referee: ....   Umpire: ....

Scorekeeper: ....

Key: C=Playing Captain   1=Point   ⊣ =Loss of Rally   ☐ =Point Scored Off Loss of Rally   △ =Libero Point

P-1=Penalty Point   P=Penalty   Px=Penalty Opponent   R=Reply   Rs=Re-Serve

T= Time-out   TX=Time-out Opponent   S=Substitution Serving Team   Sx=Opponent Substitution

If the receiving team wins the rally, it receives a point which is recorded on the line of the NEXT server's
a number and a square is drawn around it. Also draw a square around the same point on the team's running score.

Date: Home: Visitor: Set #:

Time-Outs		Game No:			First Serve (Check Box Below)		Time-Outs			

Serve Order	Player No	Team:	L:				Serve Order	Player No	Team:	L:
I					1 16 2 17	1 16 2 17	I			
II					3 18 4 19 5 20	3 18 4 19 5 20	II			
III					6 21 7 22	6 21 7 22	III			
IV					8 23 9 24 10 25	8 23 9 24 10 25	IV			
V					11 26 12 27 13 28	11 26 12 27 13 28	V			
VI					14 29 15 30	14 29 15 30	VI			
			Final Score:						Official Verification	

Subs: **1 2 3 4 5 6 7 8 9 10 11 12 13 14 15 16 17 18**   Subs: **1 2 3 4 5 6 7 8 9 10 11 12 13 14 15 16 17 18**

Comments: ....   Comments: ....

Referee: ....   Umpire: ....

Scorekeeper: ....

Key:

C=Playing Captain	1=Point	⊣ =Loss of Rally	☐ =Point Scored Off Loss of Rally	△ =Libero Point
P-1=Penalty Point	P=Penalty	Px=Penalty Opponent	R=Reply	Rs=Re-Serve
T= Time-out	TX=Time-out Opponent	S=Substitution Serving Team	Sx=Opponent Substitution	

If the receiving team wins the rally, it receives a point which is recorded on the line of the NEXT server's
a number and a square is drawn around it. Also draw a square around the same point on the team's running score.

Date: Home: Visitor: Set #:

Time-Outs		Game No:				First Serve (Check Box Below)		Time-Outs			

Serve Order	Player No	Team:			L:			Serve Order	Player No	Team:			L:
I						1 16	1 16	I					
						2 17	2 17						
II						3 18	3 18	II					
						4 19	4 19						
						5 20	5 20						
III						6 21	6 21	III					
						7 22	7 22						
						8 23	8 23						
IV						9 24	9 24	IV					
						10 25	10 25						
V						11 26	11 26	V					
						12 27	12 27						
						13 28	13 28						
VI						14 29	14 29	VI					
						15 30	15 30						

Final Score:			Official Verification	

Subs: **1 2 3 4 5 6 7 8 9 10 11 12 13 14 15 16 17 18**   Subs: **1 2 3 4 5 6 7 8 9 10 11 12 13 14 15 16 17 18**

Comments: ....   Comments: ....

....

Referee: ....   Umpire: ....

Scorekeeper: ....

Key:

C=Playing Captain	1=Point	⊣ =Loss of Rally	☐ =Point Scored Off Loss of Rally	△ =Libero Point
P-1=Penalty Point	P=Penalty	Px=Penalty Opponent	R=Reply	Rs=Re-Serve
T= Time-out	TX=Time-out Opponent	S=Substitution Serving Team	Sx=Opponent Substitution	

If the receiving team wins the rally, it receives a point which is recorded on the line of the NEXT server's
a number and a square is drawn around it. Also draw a square around the same point on the team's running score.

Date: _____ Home: _____ Visitor: _____ Set #: _____

Time-Outs		Game No:				First Serve (Check Box Below)		Time-Outs			

Serve Order	Player No	Team:						L:													Serve Order	Player No	Team:						L:									

																					1 16 / 1 16							
I									2 17 / 2 17	I		
II									3 18 / 3 18 ... 4 19 / 4 19 ... 5 20 / 5 20	II		
III									6 21 / 6 21 ... 7 22 / 7 22 ... 8 23 / 8 23	III		
IV									9 24 / 9 24 ... 10 25 / 10 25	IV		
V									11 26 / 11 26 ... 12 27 / 12 27 ... 13 28 / 13 28	V		
VI									14 29 / 14 29 ... 15 30 / 15 30	VI		

Final Score: _____   Official Verification _____

Subs: 1 2 3 4 5 6 7 8 9 10 11 12 13 14 15 16 17 18   Subs: 1 2 3 4 5 6 7 8 9 10 11 12 13 14 15 16 17 18

Comments: ....   Comments: ....

Referee: ....   Umpire: ....

Scorekeeper: ....

Key:

C=Playing Captain	1=Point	⊣ =Loss of Rally	☐ =Point Scored Off Loss of Rally	△ =Libero Point
P-1=Penalty Point	P=Penalty	Px=Penalty Opponent	R=Reply	Rs=Re-Serve
T= Time-out	TX=Time-out Opponent	S=Substitution Serving Team	Sx=Opponent Substitution	

If the receiving team wins the rally, it receives a point which is recorded on the line of the NEXT server's
a number and a square is drawn around it. Also draw a square around the same point on the team's running score.

Date: Home: Visitor: Set #:

Time-Outs		Game No:			First Serve (Check Box Below)		Time-Outs			

Serve Order	Player No	Team:	L:				Serve Order	Player No	Team:	L:
I					1 16	1 16	I			
					2 17	2 17				
II					3 18	3 18	II			
					4 19	4 19				
					5 20	5 20				
III					6 21	6 21	III			
					7 22	7 22				
					8 23	8 23				
IV					9 24	9 24	IV			
					10 25	10 25				
V					11 26	11 26	V			
					12 27	12 27				
					13 28	13 28				
VI					14 29	14 29	VI			
					15 30	15 30				
			Final Score:						Official Verification	

Subs: 1 2 3 4 5 6 7 8 9 10 11 12 13 14 15 16 17 18   Subs: 1 2 3 4 5 6 7 8 9 10 11 12 13 14 15 16 17 18

Comments: ....   Comments: ....
....

Referee: ....   Umpire: ....

Scorekeeper: ....

Key:

C=Playing Captain	1=Point	⊣ =Loss of Rally	☐ =Point Scored Off Loss of Rally	△ =Libero Point
P-1=Penalty Point	P=Penalty	Px=Penalty Opponent	R=Reply	Rs=Re-Serve
T= Time-out	TX=Time-out Opponent	S=Substitution Serving Team	Sx=Opponent Substitution	

If the receiving team wins the rally, it receives a point which is recorded on the line of the NEXT server's
a number and a square is drawn around it. Also draw a square around the same point on the team's running score.

Date:　　　　　　　Home:　　　　　　　Visitor:　　　　　　　Set #:

Time-Outs		Game No:			First Serve (Check Box Below)		Time-Outs			

Serve Order	Player No	Team:		L:			Serve Order	Player No	Team:		L:
I					1 16	1 16	I				
					2 17	2 17					
II					3 18	3 18	II				
					4 19	4 19					
					5 20	5 20					
III					6 21	6 21	III				
					7 22	7 22					
IV					8 23	8 23	IV				
					9 24	9 24					
					10 25	10 25					
V					11 26	11 26	V				
					12 27	12 27					
					13 28	13 28					
VI					14 29	14 29	VI				
					15 30	15 30					
				Final Score:						Official Verification	

Subs: 1 2 3 4 5 6 7 8 9 10 11 12 13 14 15 16 17 18　　　　　　　Subs: 1 2 3 4 5 6 7 8 9 10 11 12 13 14 15 16 17 18

Comments:　　　　　　　　　　　　　　　　　Comments:

Referee:　　　　　　　　　　　　　　　　　Umpire:

Scorekeeper:

Key:　C=Playing Captain　　1=Point　　⊣ =Loss of Rally　　□ =Point Scored Off Loss of Rally　　△ =Libero Point

P-1=Penalty Point　　P=Penalty　　Px=Penalty Opponent　　R=Reply　　Rs=Re-Serve

T= Time-out　　TX=Time-out Opponent　　S=Substitution Serving Team　　Sx=Opponent Substitution

If the receiving team wins the rally, it receives a point which is recorded on the line of the NEXT server's
a number and a square is drawn around it. Also draw a square around the same point on the team's running score.

Date: _____ Home: _____ Visitor: _____ Set #: _____

Time-Outs		Game No:				First Serve (Check Box Below)		Time-Outs			

| Serve Order | Player No | Team: | | | | | | | | | L: | | | | | | | | First Serve | | Serve Order | Player No | Team: | | | | | | | | | | L: | | | | | | | |

Serve Order	Player No	Team: L:	First Serve (left)	First Serve (right)	Serve Order	Player No	Team: L:
I			1 16 2 17	1 16 2 17	I		
II			3 18 4 19 5 20	3 18 4 19 5 20	II		
III			6 21 7 22	6 21 7 22	III		
IV			8 23 9 24 10 25	8 23 9 24 10 25	IV		
V			11 26 12 27 13 28	11 26 12 27 13 28	V		
VI			14 29 15 30	14 29 15 30	VI		
		Final Score:					Official Verification

Subs: 1 2 3 4 5 6 7 8 9 10 11 12 13 14 15 16 17 18   Subs: 1 2 3 4 5 6 7 8 9 10 11 12 13 14 15 16 17 18

Comments: ....   Comments: ....

Referee: ....   Umpire: ....

Scorekeeper: ....

Key:

C=Playing Captain	1=Point	⊣ =Loss of Rally	☐ =Point Scored Off Loss of Rally	△ =Libero Point
P-1=Penalty Point	P=Penalty	Px=Penalty Opponent	R=Reply	Rs=Re-Serve
T= Time-out	TX=Time-out Opponent	S=Substitution Serving Team	Sx=Opponent Substitution	

If the receiving team wins the rally, it receives a point which is recorded on the line of the NEXT server's
a number and a square is drawn around it. Also draw a square around the same point on the team's running score.

Date: Home: Visitor: Set #:

Time-Outs		Game No:				First Serve (Check Box Below)		Time-Outs			
Serve Order	Player No	Team:		L:				Serve Order	Player No	Team:	L:
I						1 16 / 2 17	1 16 / 2 17	I			
II						3 18 / 4 19 / 5 20	3 18 / 4 19 / 5 20	II			
III						6 21 / 7 22	6 21 / 7 22	III			
IV						8 23 / 9 24 / 10 25	8 23 / 9 24 / 10 25	IV			
V						11 26 / 12 27 / 13 28	11 26 / 12 27 / 13 28	V			
VI						14 29 / 15 30	14 29 / 15 30	VI			
			Final Score:							Official Verification	

Subs: 1 2 3 4 5 6 7 8 9 10 11 12 13 14 15 16 17 18   Subs: 1 2 3 4 5 6 7 8 9 10 11 12 13 14 15 16 17 18

Comments: ....   Comments: ....

Referee: ....   Umpire: ....

Scorekeeper: ....

Key:

C=Playing Captain	1=Point	⊣ =Loss of Rally	☐ =Point Scored Off Loss of Rally	△ =Libero Point
P-1=Penalty Point	P=Penalty	Px=Penalty Opponent	R=Reply	Rs=Re-Serve
T= Time-out	TX=Time-out Opponent	S=Substitution Serving Team	Sx=Opponent Substitution	

If the receiving team wins the rally, it receives a point which is recorded on the line of the NEXT server's
a number and a square is drawn around it. Also draw a square around the same point on the team's running score.

Date: Home: Visitor: Set #:

Time-Outs		Game No:			First Serve (Check Box Below)		Time-Outs			

Serve Order	Player No	Team:			L:				Serve Order	Player No	Team:		L:
I						1 16	1 16		I				
						2 17	2 17						
II						3 18	3 18		II				
						4 19	4 19						
						5 20	5 20						
III						6 21	6 21		III				
						7 22	7 22						
IV						8 23	8 23		IV				
						9 24	9 24						
						10 25	10 25						
V						11 26	11 26		V				
						12 27	12 27						
						13 28	13 28						
VI						14 29	14 29		VI				
						15 30	15 30						

Final Score: | | Official Verification

Subs: 1 2 3 4 5 6 7 8 9 10 11 12 13 14 15 16 17 18

Subs: 1 2 3 4 5 6 7 8 9 10 11 12 13 14 15 16 17 18

Comments: ....

Comments: ....

Referee: ....

Umpire: ....

Scorekeeper: ....

Key:

C=Playing Captain	1=Point	⊣ =Loss of Rally	☐ =Point Scored Off Loss of Rally	△ =Libero Point
P-1=Penalty Point	P=Penalty	Px=Penalty Opponent	R=Reply	Rs=Re-Serve
T= Time-out	TX=Time-out Opponent	S=Substitution Serving Team	Sx=Opponent Substitution	

If the receiving team wins the rally, it receives a point which is recorded on the line of the NEXT server's
a number and a square is drawn around it. Also draw a square around the same point on the team's running score.

Date: Home: Visitor: Set #:

Time-Outs		Game No:				First Serve (Check Box Below)		Time-Outs				

Serve Order	Player No	Team:										L:										Serve Order	Player No	Team:									L:								

First Serve center columns:

1 16	1 16
2 17	2 17
3 18	3 18
4 19	4 19
5 20	5 20
6 21	6 21
7 22	7 22
8 23	8 23
9 24	9 24
10 25	10 25
11 26	11 26
12 27	12 27
13 28	13 28
14 29	14 29
15 30	15 30

Serve Order: I, II, III, IV, V, VI (both left and right sides)

Final Score: | | Official Verification

Subs: 1 2 3 4 5 6 7 8 9 10 11 12 13 14 15 16 17 18   Subs: 1 2 3 4 5 6 7 8 9 10 11 12 13 14 15 16 17 18

Comments: ....   Comments: ....
....

Referee: ....   Umpire: ....

Scorekeeper: ....

Key:

C=Playing Captain	1=Point	⊣ =Loss of Rally	☐ =Point Scored Off Loss of Rally	△ =Libero Point
P-1=Penalty Point	P=Penalty	Px=Penalty Opponent	R=Reply	Rs=Re-Serve
T= Time-out	TX=Time-out Opponent	S=Substitution Serving Team	Sx=Opponent Substitution	

If the receiving team wins the rally, it receives a point which is recorded on the line of the NEXT server's
a number and a square is drawn around it. Also draw a square around the same point on the team's running score.

Date: Home: Visitor: Set #:

Time-Outs		Game No:				First Serve (Check Box Below)		Time-Outs			

Serve Order	Player No	Team:				L:				Serve Order	Player No	Team:				L:

I								1 16	1 16	I
								2 17	2 17	
II								3 18	3 18	II
								4 19	4 19	
								5 20	5 20	
III								6 21	6 21	III
								7 22	7 22	
								8 23	8 23	
IV								9 24	9 24	IV
								10 25	10 25	
V								11 26	11 26	V
								12 27	12 27	
								13 28	13 28	
VI								14 29	14 29	VI
								15 30	15 30	

Final Score: Official Verification

Subs: 1 2 3 4 5 6 7 8 9 10 11 12 13 14 15 16 17 18   Subs: 1 2 3 4 5 6 7 8 9 10 11 12 13 14 15 16 17 18

Comments: ....   Comments: ....

Referee: ....   Umpire: ....

Scorekeeper: ....

Key:

C=Playing Captain	1=Point	⊣ =Loss of Rally	□ =Point Scored Off Loss of Rally	△ =Libero Point
P-1=Penalty Point	P=Penalty	Px=Penalty Opponent	R=Reply	Rs=Re-Serve
T= Time-out	TX=Time-out Opponent	S=Substitution Serving Team	Sx=Opponent Substitution	

If the receiving team wins the rally, it receives a point which is recorded on the line of the NEXT server's
a number and a square is drawn around it. Also draw a square around the same point on the team's running score.

Date: Home: Visitor: Set #:

<table>
<tr><td colspan="2">Time-Outs</td><td rowspan="2">Game No:</td><td></td><td colspan="2">First Serve
(Check Box Below)</td><td colspan="2">Time-Outs</td><td></td></tr>
<tr><td></td><td></td><td></td><td></td><td></td><td></td><td></td><td></td></tr>
<tr><td>Serve Order</td><td>Player No</td><td colspan="2">Team: L:</td><td></td><td></td><td>Serve Order</td><td>Player No</td><td colspan="2">Team: L:</td></tr>
<tr><td>I</td><td></td><td></td><td></td><td>1 16
2 17</td><td>1 16
2 17</td><td>I</td><td></td><td></td><td></td></tr>
<tr><td>II</td><td></td><td></td><td></td><td>3 18
4 19
5 20</td><td>3 18
4 19
5 20</td><td>II</td><td></td><td></td><td></td></tr>
<tr><td>III</td><td></td><td></td><td></td><td>6 21
7 22
8 23</td><td>6 21
7 22
8 23</td><td>III</td><td></td><td></td><td></td></tr>
<tr><td>IV</td><td></td><td></td><td></td><td>9 24
10 25</td><td>9 24
10 25</td><td>IV</td><td></td><td></td><td></td></tr>
<tr><td>V</td><td></td><td></td><td></td><td>11 26
12 27
13 28</td><td>11 26
12 27
13 28</td><td>V</td><td></td><td></td><td></td></tr>
<tr><td>VI</td><td></td><td></td><td></td><td>14 29
15 30</td><td>14 29
15 30</td><td>VI</td><td></td><td></td><td></td></tr>
<tr><td colspan="4">Final Score:</td><td></td><td></td><td colspan="4">Official Verification</td></tr>
</table>

Subs: 1 2 3 4 5 6 7 8 9 10 11 12 13 14 15 16 17 18   Subs: 1 2 3 4 5 6 7 8 9 10 11 12 13 14 15 16 17 18

Comments: ....   Comments: ....

Referee: ....   Umpire: ....

Scorekeeper: ....

Key:

C=Playing Captain	1=Point	⊣ =Loss of Rally	☐ =Point Scored Off Loss of Rally	△ =Libero Point
P-1=Penalty Point	P=Penalty	Px=Penalty Opponent	R=Reply	Rs=Re-Serve
T= Time-out	TX=Time-out Opponent	S=Substitution Serving Team	Sx=Opponent Substitution	

If the receiving team wins the rally, it receives a point which is recorded on the line of the NEXT server's
a number and a square is drawn around it. Also draw a square around the same point on the team's running score.

Date: Home: Visitor: Set #:

Time-Outs		Game No:			First Serve (Check Box Below)		Time-Outs			

Serve Order	Player No	Team:	L:				Serve Order	Player No	Team:	L:
I					1 16 / 2 17	1 16 / 2 17	I			
II					3 18 / 4 19 / 5 20	3 18 / 4 19 / 5 20	II			
III					6 21 / 7 22	6 21 / 7 22	III			
IV					8 23 / 9 24 / 10 25	8 23 / 9 24 / 10 25	IV			
V					11 26 / 12 27 / 13 28	11 26 / 12 27 / 13 28	V			
VI					14 29 / 15 30	14 29 / 15 30	VI			
		Final Score:							Official Verification	

Subs: 1 2 3 4 5 6 7 8 9 10 11 12 13 14 15 16 17 18   Subs: 1 2 3 4 5 6 7 8 9 10 11 12 13 14 15 16 17 18

Comments: ....   Comments: ....

Referee: ....   Umpire: ....

Scorekeeper: ....

Key:

C=Playing Captain	1=Point	⊣ =Loss of Rally	☐ =Point Scored Off Loss of Rally	△ =Libero Point
P-1=Penalty Point	P=Penalty	Px=Penalty Opponent	R=Reply	Rs=Re-Serve
T= Time-out	TX=Time-out Opponent	S=Substitution Serving Team	Sx=Opponent Substitution	

If the receiving team wins the rally, it receives a point which is recorded on the line of the NEXT server's
a number and a square is drawn around it. Also draw a square around the same point on the team's running score.

Date:	Home:	Visitor:	Set #:

Time-Outs		Game No:							First Serve (Check Box Below)		Time-Outs								

| Serve Order | Player No | Team: | | | | | | | L: | | | | | Serve Order | Player No | Team: | | | | | | L: |

Home side serve order: I, II, III, IV, V, VI

First Serve center columns:
1 16	1 16
2 17	2 17
3 18	3 18
4 19	4 19
5 20	5 20
6 21	6 21
7 22	7 22
8 23	8 23
9 24	9 24
10 25	10 25
11 26	11 26
12 27	12 27
13 28	13 28
14 29	14 29
15 30	15 30

Visitor side serve order: I, II, III, IV, V, VI

Final Score: _____ | Official Verification _____

Subs: 1 2 3 4 5 6 7 8 9 10 11 12 13 14 15 16 17 18

Comments: ....

Referee: ....

Scorekeeper: ....

Subs: 1 2 3 4 5 6 7 8 9 10 11 12 13 14 15 16 17 18

Comments: ....

Umpire: ....

Key:
- C=Playing Captain
- 1=Point
- ⊣ =Loss of Rally
- □ =Point Scored Off Loss of Rally
- △ =Libero Point
- P-1=Penalty Point
- P=Penalty
- Px=Penalty Opponent
- R=Reply
- Rs=Re-Serve
- T= Time-out
- TX=Time-out Opponent
- S=Substitution Serving Team
- Sx=Opponent Substitution

If the receiving team wins the rally, it receives a point which is recorded on the line of the NEXT server's a number and a square is drawn around it. Also draw a square around the same point on the team's running score.

Date: Home: Visitor: Set #:

Time-Outs		Game No:			First Serve (Check Box Below)		Time-Outs			

Serve Order	Player No	Team:		L:			Serve Order	Player No	Team:		L:
I					1 16	1 16	I				
					2 17	2 17					
II					3 18	3 18	II				
					4 19	4 19					
					5 20	5 20					
III					6 21	6 21	III				
					7 22	7 22					
					8 23	8 23					
IV					9 24	9 24	IV				
					10 25	10 25					
V					11 26	11 26	V				
					12 27	12 27					
					13 28	13 28					
VI					14 29	14 29	VI				
					15 30	15 30					
			Final Score:							Official Verification	

Subs: 1 2 3 4 5 6 7 8 9 10 11 12 13 14 15 16 17 18   Subs: 1 2 3 4 5 6 7 8 9 10 11 12 13 14 15 16 17 18

Comments: ....   Comments: ....

....

Referee: ....   Umpire: ....

Scorekeeper: ....

Key:

C=Playing Captain	1=Point	⊣ =Loss of Rally	☐ =Point Scored Off Loss of Rally	△ =Libero Point
P-1=Penalty Point	P=Penalty	Px=Penalty Opponent	R=Reply	Rs=Re-Serve
T= Time-out	TX=Time-out Opponent	S=Substitution Serving Team	Sx=Opponent Substitution	

If the receiving team wins the rally, it receives a point which is recorded on the line of the NEXT server's
a number and a square is drawn around it. Also draw a square around the same point on the team's running score.

Date: Home: Visitor: Set #:

Time-Outs		Game No:						First Serve (Check Box Below)		Time-Outs			
Serve Order	Player No	Team:					L:			Serve Order	Player No	Team:	L:
I								1 16 2 17	1 16 2 17	I			
II								3 18 4 19 5 20	3 18 4 19 5 20	II			
III								6 21 7 22 8 23	6 21 7 22 8 23	III			
IV								9 24 10 25	9 24 10 25	IV			
V								11 26 12 27 13 28	11 26 12 27 13 28	V			
VI								14 29 15 30	14 29 15 30	VI			
					Final Score:							Official Verification	

Subs: 1 2 3 4 5 6 7 8 9 10 11 12 13 14 15 16 17 18   Subs: 1 2 3 4 5 6 7 8 9 10 11 12 13 14 15 16 17 18

Comments: ....   Comments: ....

Referee: ....   Umpire: ....

Scorekeeper: ....

Key:

C=Playing Captain	1=Point	⊣ =Loss of Rally	□ =Point Scored Off Loss of Rally	△ =Libero Point
P-1=Penalty Point	P=Penalty	Px=Penalty Opponent	R=Reply	Rs=Re-Serve
T= Time-out	TX=Time-out Opponent	S=Substitution Serving Team	Sx=Opponent Substitution	

If the receiving team wins the rally, it receives a point which is recorded on the line of the NEXT server's
a number and a square is drawn around it. Also draw a square around the same point on the team's running score.

Date: Home: Visitor: Set #:

Time-Outs		Game No:			First Serve (Check Box Below)		Time-Outs			

Serve Order	Player No	Team:		L:			Serve Order	Player No	Team:		L:
I					1 16 2 17	1 16 2 17	I				
II					3 18 4 19 5 20	3 18 4 19 5 20	II				
III					6 21 7 22 8 23	6 21 7 22 8 23	III				
IV					9 24 10 25	9 24 10 25	IV				
V					11 26 12 27 13 28	11 26 12 27 13 28	V				
VI					14 29 15 30	14 29 15 30	VI				
			Final Score:						Official Verification		

Subs: 1 2 3 4 5 6 7 8 9 10 11 12 13 14 15 16 17 18   Subs: 1 2 3 4 5 6 7 8 9 10 11 12 13 14 15 16 17 18

Comments: ....   Comments: ....

Referee: ....   Umpire: ....

Scorekeeper: ....

Key: C=Playing Captain   1=Point   ⊣ =Loss of Rally   ☐ =Point Scored Off Loss of Rally   △ =Libero Point

P-1=Penalty Point   P=Penalty   Px=Penalty Opponent   R=Reply   Rs=Re-Serve

T= Time-out   TX=Time-out Opponent   S=Substitution Serving Team   Sx=Opponent Substitution

If the receiving team wins the rally, it receives a point which is recorded on the line of the NEXT server's
a number and a square is drawn around it. Also draw a square around the same point on the team's running score.

Date: Home: Visitor: Set #:

Time-Outs		Game No:		First Serve (Check Box Below)		Time-Outs		

Serve Order	Player No	Team:	L:			Serve Order	Player No	Team:	L:
I				1 16 / 2 17	1 16 / 2 17	I			
II				3 18 / 4 19 / 5 20	3 18 / 4 19 / 5 20	II			
III				6 21 / 7 22	6 21 / 7 22	III			
IV				8 23 / 9 24 / 10 25	8 23 / 9 24 / 10 25	IV			
V				11 26 / 12 27 / 13 28	11 26 / 12 27 / 13 28	V			
VI				14 29 / 15 30	14 29 / 15 30	VI			
Final Score:						Official Verification			

Subs: 1 2 3 4 5 6 7 8 9 10 11 12 13 14 15 16 17 18   Subs: 1 2 3 4 5 6 7 8 9 10 11 12 13 14 15 16 17 18

Comments: ....   Comments: ....

Referee: ....   Umpire: ....

Scorekeeper: ....

Key:

C=Playing Captain	1=Point	⊣ =Loss of Rally	☐ =Point Scored Off Loss of Rally	△ =Libero Point
P-1=Penalty Point	P=Penalty	Px=Penalty Opponent	R=Reply	Rs=Re-Serve
T= Time-out	TX=Time-out Opponent	S=Substitution Serving Team	Sx=Opponent Substitution	

If the receiving team wins the rally, it receives a point which is recorded on the line of the NEXT server's
a number and a square is drawn around it. Also draw a square around the same point on the team's running score.

Date: Home: Visitor: Set #:

Time-Outs		Game No:					First Serve (Check Box Below)		Time-Outs			

Serve Order	Player No	Team: L:							Serve Order	Player No	Team: L:	
I							1 16 2 17	1 16 2 17	I			
II							3 18 4 19 5 20	3 18 4 19 5 20	II			
III							6 21 7 22	6 21 7 22	III			
IV							8 23 9 24 10 25	8 23 9 24 10 25	IV			
V							11 26 12 27 13 28	11 26 12 27 13 28	V			
VI							14 29 15 30	14 29 15 30	VI			

Final Score: Official Verification

Subs: 1 2 3 4 5 6 7 8 9 10 11 12 13 14 15 16 17 18   Subs: 1 2 3 4 5 6 7 8 9 10 11 12 13 14 15 16 17 18

Comments: ....   Comments: ....

Referee: ....   Umpire: ....

Scorekeeper: ....

Key:

C=Playing Captain	1=Point	⊣ =Loss of Rally	☐ =Point Scored Off Loss of Rally	△ =Libero Point
P-1=Penalty Point	P=Penalty	Px=Penalty Opponent	R=Reply	Rs=Re-Serve
T= Time-out	TX=Time-out Opponent	S=Substitution Serving Team	Sx=Opponent Substitution	

If the receiving team wins the rally, it receives a point which is recorded on the line of the NEXT server's
a number and a square is drawn around it. Also draw a square around the same point on the team's running score.

Date: _____ Home: _____ Visitor: _____ Set #: _____

	Time-Outs		Game No:			First Serve (Check Box Below)		Time-Outs			

Serve Order	Player No	Team:	L:					Serve Order	Player No	Team:	L:
I						1 16 / 2 17	1 16 / 2 17	I			
II						3 18 / 4 19 / 5 20	3 18 / 4 19 / 5 20	II			
III						6 21 / 7 22	6 21 / 7 22	III			
IV						8 23 / 9 24 / 10 25	8 23 / 9 24 / 10 25	IV			
V						11 26 / 12 27 / 13 28	11 26 / 12 27 / 13 28	V			
VI						14 29 / 15 30	14 29 / 15 30	VI			

Final Score: _____ | Official Verification _____

Subs: 1 2 3 4 5 6 7 8 9 10 11 12 13 14 15 16 17 18   Subs: 1 2 3 4 5 6 7 8 9 10 11 12 13 14 15 16 17 18

Comments: ....   Comments: ....

Referee: ....   Umpire: ....

Scorekeeper: ....

Key:
C=Playing Captain	1=Point	⊣ =Loss of Rally	□ =Point Scored Off Loss of Rally	△ =Libero Point
P-1=Penalty Point	P=Penalty	Px=Penalty Opponent	R=Reply	Rs=Re-Serve
T= Time-out	TX=Time-out Opponent	S=Substitution Serving Team	Sx=Opponent Substitution	

If the receiving team wins the rally, it receives a point which is recorded on the line of the NEXT server's
a number and a square is drawn around it. Also draw a square around the same point on the team's running score.

Date: Home: Visitor: Set #:

Time-Outs		Game No:			First Serve (Check Box Below)		Time-Outs			

Serve Order	Player No	Team:				L:			Serve Order	Player No	Team:		L:
I							1 16	1 16	I				
							2 17	2 17					
II							3 18	3 18	II				
							4 19	4 19					
							5 20	5 20					
III							6 21	6 21	III				
							7 22	7 22					
							8 23	8 23					
IV							9 24	9 24	IV				
							10 25	10 25					
V							11 26	11 26	V				
							12 27	12 27					
							13 28	13 28					
VI							14 29	14 29	VI				
							15 30	15 30					
					Final Score:							Official Verification	

Subs: 1 2 3 4 5 6 7 8 9 10 11 12 13 14 15 16 17 18   Subs: 1 2 3 4 5 6 7 8 9 10 11 12 13 14 15 16 17 18

Comments: ....   Comments: ....

Referee: ....   Umpire: ....

Scorekeeper: ....

Key:

C=Playing Captain	1=Point	⊣ =Loss of Rally	☐ =Point Scored Off Loss of Rally	△ =Libero Point
P-1=Penalty Point	P=Penalty	Px=Penalty Opponent	R=Reply	Rs=Re-Serve
T= Time-out	TX=Time-out Opponent	S=Substitution Serving Team	Sx=Opponent Substitution	

If the receiving team wins the rally, it receives a point which is recorded on the line of the NEXT server's
a number and a square is drawn around it. Also draw a square around the same point on the team's running score.

Date: Home: Visitor: Set #:

Time-Outs		Game No:					First Serve (Check Box Below)		Time-Outs				

Serve Order	Player No	Team:				L:				Serve Order	Player No	Team:				L:
I							1 16	1 16		I						
							2 17	2 17								
II							3 18	3 18		II						
							4 19	4 19								
							5 20	5 20								
III							6 21	6 21		III						
							7 22	7 22								
							8 23	8 23								
IV							9 24	9 24		IV						
							10 25	10 25								
V							11 26	11 26		V						
							12 27	12 27								
							13 28	13 28								
VI							14 29	14 29		VI						
							15 30	15 30								
					Final Score:								Official Verification			

Subs: 1 2 3 4 5 6 7 8 9 10 11 12 13 14 15 16 17 18   Subs: 1 2 3 4 5 6 7 8 9 10 11 12 13 14 15 16 17 18

Comments: ....   Comments: ....

Referee: ....   Umpire: ....

Scorekeeper: ....

Key:
- C=Playing Captain
- 1=Point
- ⊣ =Loss of Rally
- ☐ =Point Scored Off Loss of Rally
- △ =Libero Point
- P-1=Penalty Point
- P=Penalty
- Px=Penalty Opponent
- R=Reply
- Rs=Re-Serve
- T= Time-out
- TX=Time-out Opponent
- S=Substitution Serving Team
- Sx=Opponent Substitution

If the receiving team wins the rally, it receives a point which is recorded on the line of the NEXT server's
a number and a square is drawn around it. Also draw a square around the same point on the team's running score.

Date: Home: Visitor: Set #:

Time-Outs		Game No:			First Serve (Check Box Below)		Time-Outs			

Serve Order	Player No	Team:			L:				Serve Order	Player No	Team:			L:

Serve Order	Player No	Team / L row	First Serve col 1	First Serve col 2	Serve Order	Player No	Team / L row
I			1 16 / 2 17	1 16 / 2 17	I		
II			3 18 / 4 19 / 5 20	3 18 / 4 19 / 5 20	II		
III			6 21 / 7 22	6 21 / 7 22	III		
IV			8 23 / 9 24 / 10 25	8 23 / 9 24 / 10 25	IV		
V			11 26 / 12 27 / 13 28	11 26 / 12 27 / 13 28	V		
VI			14 29 / 15 30	14 29 / 15 30	VI		

Final Score: | | Official Verification

Subs: 1 2 3 4 5 6 7 8 9 10 11 12 13 14 15 16 17 18   Subs: 1 2 3 4 5 6 7 8 9 10 11 12 13 14 15 16 17 18

Comments: ....   Comments: ....
....

Referee: ....   Umpire: ....

Scorekeeper: ....

Key:

C=Playing Captain	1=Point	⊣ =Loss of Rally	☐ =Point Scored Off Loss of Rally	△ =Libero Point
P-1=Penalty Point	P=Penalty	Px=Penalty Opponent	R=Reply	Rs=Re-Serve
T= Time-out	TX=Time-out Opponent	S=Substitution Serving Team	Sx=Opponent Substitution	

If the receiving team wins the rally, it receives a point which is recorded on the line of the NEXT server's
a number and a square is drawn around it. Also draw a square around the same point on the team's running score.

Date: Home: Visitor: Set #:

Time-Outs		Game No:		First Serve (Check Box Below)		Time-Outs		

Serve Order	Player No	Team:	L:			Serve Order	Player No	Team:	L:
I				1 16	1 16	I			
II				2 17 3 18 4 19	2 17 3 18 4 19	II			
III				5 20 6 21 7 22	5 20 6 21 7 22	III			
IV				8 23 9 24 10 25	8 23 9 24 10 25	IV			
V				11 26 12 27 13 28	11 26 12 27 13 28	V			
VI				14 29 15 30	14 29 15 30	VI			
			Final Score:					Official Verification	

Subs: 1 2 3 4 5 6 7 8 9 10 11 12 13 14 15 16 17 18   Subs: 1 2 3 4 5 6 7 8 9 10 11 12 13 14 15 16 17 18

Comments: ....   Comments: ....

Referee: ....   Umpire: ....

Scorekeeper: ....

Key:

C=Playing Captain	1=Point	⊣ =Loss of Rally	☐ =Point Scored Off Loss of Rally	△ =Libero Point
P-1=Penalty Point	P=Penalty	Px=Penalty Opponent	R=Reply	Rs=Re-Serve
T= Time-out	TX=Time-out Opponent	S=Substitution Serving Team	Sx=Opponent Substitution	

If the receiving team wins the rally, it receives a point which is recorded on the line of the NEXT server's
a number and a square is drawn around it. Also draw a square around the same point on the team's running score.

Date: Home: Visitor: Set #:

Time-Outs		Game No:			First Serve (Check Box Below)		Time-Outs			

Serve Order	Player No	Team:				L:			Serve Order	Player No	Team:			L:

Serve Order				First Serve boxes		Serve Order	
I			1 16 / 2 17	1 16 / 2 17		I	
II			3 18 / 4 19 / 5 20	3 18 / 4 19 / 5 20		II	
III			6 21 / 7 22 / 8 23	6 21 / 7 22 / 8 23		III	
IV			9 24 / 10 25	9 24 / 10 25		IV	
V			11 26 / 12 27 / 13 28	11 26 / 12 27 / 13 28		V	
VI			14 29 / 15 30	14 29 / 15 30		VI	

Final Score: Official Verification

Subs: 1 2 3 4 5 6 7 8 9 10 11 12 13 14 15 16 17 18   Subs: 1 2 3 4 5 6 7 8 9 10 11 12 13 14 15 16 17 18

Comments: ....   Comments: ....

Referee: ....   Umpire: ....

Scorekeeper: ....

Key:

C=Playing Captain	1=Point	⊣ =Loss of Rally	☐ =Point Scored Off Loss of Rally	△ =Libero Point
P-1=Penalty Point	P=Penalty	Px=Penalty Opponent	R=Reply	Rs=Re-Serve
T= Time-out	TX=Time-out Opponent	S=Substitution Serving Team	Sx=Opponent Substitution	

If the receiving team wins the rally, it receives a point which is recorded on the line of the NEXT server's
a number and a square is drawn around it. Also draw a square around the same point on the team's running score.

Date: Home: Visitor: Set #:

Time-Outs		Game No:			First Serve (Check Box Below)		Time-Outs			

Serve Order	Player No	Team:				L:			Serve Order	Player No	Team:			L:

First Serve (Check Box Below):

1 16	1 16
2 17	2 17
3 18	3 18
4 19	4 19
5 20	5 20
6 21	6 21
7 22	7 22
8 23	8 23
9 24	9 24
10 25	10 25
11 26	11 26
12 27	12 27
13 28	13 28
14 29	14 29
15 30	15 30

Serve Order (left): I, II, III, IV, V, VI
Serve Order (right): I, II, III, IV, V, VI

Final Score: Official Verification

Subs: 1 2 3 4 5 6 7 8 9 10 11 12 13 14 15 16 17 18   Subs: 1 2 3 4 5 6 7 8 9 10 11 12 13 14 15 16 17 18

Comments: ....   Comments: ....

Referee: ....   Umpire: ....

Scorekeeper: ....

Key:

C=Playing Captain	1=Point	⊣ =Loss of Rally	☐ =Point Scored Off Loss of Rally	△ =Libero Point
P-1=Penalty Point	P=Penalty	Px=Penalty Opponent	R=Reply	Rs=Re-Serve
T= Time-out	TX=Time-out Opponent	S=Substitution Serving Team	Sx=Opponent Substitution	

If the receiving team wins the rally, it receives a point which is recorded on the line of the NEXT server's
a number and a square is drawn around it. Also draw a square around the same point on the team's running score.

Date: Home: Visitor: Set #:

Time-Outs		Game No:			First Serve (Check Box Below)			Time-Outs			

Serve Order	Player No	Team:				L:				Serve Order	Player No	Team:				L:

Serve Order				First Serve		Serve Order	
I				1 16	1 16	I	
				2 17	2 17		
II				3 18	3 18	II	
				4 19	4 19		
				5 20	5 20		
III				6 21	6 21	III	
				7 22	7 22		
				8 23	8 23		
IV				9 24	9 24	IV	
				10 25	10 25		
V				11 26	11 26	V	
				12 27	12 27		
				13 28	13 28		
VI				14 29	14 29	VI	
				15 30	15 30		

Final Score: Official Verification

Subs: 1 2 3 4 5 6 7 8 9 10 11 12 13 14 15 16 17 18   Subs: 1 2 3 4 5 6 7 8 9 10 11 12 13 14 15 16 17 18

Comments: ....   Comments: ....

Referee: ....   Umpire: ....

Scorekeeper: ....

Key:
C=Playing Captain	1=Point	⊣ =Loss of Rally	☐ =Point Scored Off Loss of Rally	△ =Libero Point
P-1=Penalty Point	P=Penalty	Px=Penalty Opponent	R=Reply	Rs=Re-Serve
T= Time-out	TX=Time-out Opponent	S=Substitution Serving Team	Sx=Opponent Substitution	

If the receiving team wins the rally, it receives a point which is recorded on the line of the NEXT server's
a number and a square is drawn around it. Also draw a square around the same point on the team's running score.

Date: Home: Visitor: Set #:

Time-Outs		Game No:		First Serve (Check Box Below)		Time-Outs		

Serve Order	Player No	Team:	L:			Serve Order	Player No	Team:	L:
I				1 16	1 16	I			
II				2 17 / 3 18	2 17 / 3 18	II			
III				4 19 / 5 20 / 6 21 / 7 22	4 19 / 5 20 / 6 21 / 7 22	III			
IV				8 23 / 9 24 / 10 25	8 23 / 9 24 / 10 25	IV			
V				11 26 / 12 27 / 13 28	11 26 / 12 27 / 13 28	V			
VI				14 29 / 15 30	14 29 / 15 30	VI			
		Final Score:						Official Verification	

Subs: 1 2 3 4 5 6 7 8 9 10 11 12 13 14 15 16 17 18   Subs: 1 2 3 4 5 6 7 8 9 10 11 12 13 14 15 16 17 18

Comments: ....   Comments: ....

Referee: ....   Umpire: ....

Scorekeeper: ....

Key:
C=Playing Captain	1=Point	⊣ =Loss of Rally	☐ =Point Scored Off Loss of Rally	△ =Libero Point
P-1=Penalty Point	P=Penalty	Px=Penalty Opponent	R=Reply	Rs=Re-Serve
T= Time-out	TX=Time-out Opponent	S=Substitution Serving Team	Sx=Opponent Substitution	

If the receiving team wins the rally, it receives a point which is recorded on the line of the NEXT server's
a number and a square is drawn around it. Also draw a square around the same point on the team's running score.

Date: Home: Visitor: Set #:

<table>
<tr><td colspan="2">Time-Outs</td><td rowspan="2">Game No:</td><td colspan="2">First Serve
(Check Box Below)</td><td colspan="2">Time-Outs</td><td></td></tr>
<tr><td></td><td></td><td></td><td></td><td></td><td></td><td></td></tr>
<tr><td>Serve
Order</td><td>Player
No</td><td colspan="2">Team: L:</td><td></td><td></td><td>Serve
Order</td><td>Player
No</td><td colspan="2">Team: L:</td></tr>
<tr><td>I</td><td></td><td></td><td></td><td>1 16
2 17</td><td>1 16
2 17</td><td>I</td><td></td><td></td><td></td></tr>
<tr><td>II</td><td></td><td></td><td></td><td>3 18
4 19
5 20</td><td>3 18
4 19
5 20</td><td>II</td><td></td><td></td><td></td></tr>
<tr><td>III</td><td></td><td></td><td></td><td>6 21
7 22</td><td>6 21
7 22</td><td>III</td><td></td><td></td><td></td></tr>
<tr><td>IV</td><td></td><td></td><td></td><td>8 23
9 24
10 25</td><td>8 23
9 24
10 25</td><td>IV</td><td></td><td></td><td></td></tr>
<tr><td>V</td><td></td><td></td><td></td><td>11 26
12 27
13 28</td><td>11 26
12 27
13 28</td><td>V</td><td></td><td></td><td></td></tr>
<tr><td>VI</td><td></td><td></td><td></td><td>14 29
15 30</td><td>14 29
15 30</td><td>VI</td><td></td><td></td><td></td></tr>
<tr><td colspan="4">Final Score:</td><td></td><td></td><td colspan="4">Official Verification</td></tr>
</table>

Subs: 1 2 3 4 5 6 7 8 9 10 11 12 13 14 15 16 17 18   Subs: 1 2 3 4 5 6 7 8 9 10 11 12 13 14 15 16 17 18

Comments: ....   Comments: ....
....

Referee: ....   Umpire: ....

Scorekeeper: ....

Key:
C=Playing Captain	1=Point	⊣ =Loss of Rally	☐ =Point Scored Off Loss of Rally	△ =Libero Point
P-1=Penalty Point	P=Penalty	Px=Penalty Opponent	R=Reply	Rs=Re-Serve
T= Time-out	TX=Time-out Opponent	S=Substitution Serving Team	Sx=Opponent Substitution	

If the receiving team wins the rally, it receives a point which is recorded on the line of the NEXT server's
a number and a square is drawn around it. Also draw a square around the same point on the team's running score.

Date: Home: Visitor: Set #:

Time-Outs		Game No:			First Serve (Check Box Below)		Time-Outs		Team:	L:

Serve Order	Player No	Team:		L:			Serve Order	Player No	Team:		L:

I					1 16	1 16	I			
					2 17	2 17				
II					3 18	3 18	II			
					4 19	4 19				
					5 20	5 20				
III					6 21	6 21	III			
					7 22	7 22				
					8 23	8 23				
IV					9 24	9 24	IV			
					10 25	10 25				
					11 26	11 26				
V					12 27	12 27	V			
					13 28	13 28				
VI					14 29	14 29	VI			
					15 30	15 30				

Final Score: Official Verification

Subs: 1 2 3 4 5 6 7 8 9 10 11 12 13 14 15 16 17 18   Subs: 1 2 3 4 5 6 7 8 9 10 11 12 13 14 15 16 17 18

Comments: ....   Comments: ....

Referee: ....   Umpire: ....

Scorekeeper: ....

Key:

C=Playing Captain	1=Point	⊣ =Loss of Rally	☐ =Point Scored Off Loss of Rally	△ =Libero Point
P-1=Penalty Point	P=Penalty	Px=Penalty Opponent	R=Reply	Rs=Re-Serve
T= Time-out	TX=Time-out Opponent	S=Substitution Serving Team	Sx=Opponent Substitution	

If the receiving team wins the rally, it receives a point which is recorded on the line of the NEXT server's
a number and a square is drawn around it. Also draw a square around the same point on the team's running score.

Date: Home: Visitor: Set #:

Time-Outs		Game No:				First Serve (Check Box Below)		Time-Outs			

Serve Order	Player No	Team:								L:												Serve Order	Player No	Team:				L:											

Serve order rows: I, II, III, IV, V, VI (both left and right sides)

First Serve check box numbers:
1 16	1 16
2 17	2 17
3 18	3 18
4 19	4 19
5 20	5 20
6 21	6 21
7 22	7 22
8 23	8 23
9 24	9 24
10 25	10 25
11 26	11 26
12 27	12 27
13 28	13 28
14 29	14 29
15 30	15 30

Final Score: Official Verification

Subs: 1 2 3 4 5 6 7 8 9 10 11 12 13 14 15 16 17 18   Subs: 1 2 3 4 5 6 7 8 9 10 11 12 13 14 15 16 17 18

Comments: ....   Comments: ....

Referee: ....   Umpire: ....

Scorekeeper: ....

Key:
C=Playing Captain	1=Point	⊣ =Loss of Rally	☐ =Point Scored Off Loss of Rally	△ =Libero Point
P-1=Penalty Point	P=Penalty	Px=Penalty Opponent	R=Reply	Rs=Re-Serve
T= Time-out	TX=Time-out Opponent	S=Substitution Serving Team	Sx=Opponent Substitution	

If the receiving team wins the rally, it receives a point which is recorded on the line of the NEXT server's
a number and a square is drawn around it. Also draw a square around the same point on the team's running score.

Date: _____ Home: _____ Visitor: _____ Set #: _____

Time-Outs		Game No:		First Serve (Check Box Below)		Time-Outs			

Serve Order	Player No	Team:	L:			Serve Order	Player No	Team:	L:
I				1 16	1 16	I			
				2 17	2 17				
II				3 18	3 18	II			
				4 19	4 19				
				5 20	5 20				
III				6 21	6 21	III			
				7 22	7 22				
				8 23	8 23				
IV				9 24	9 24	IV			
				10 25	10 25				
				11 26	11 26				
V				12 27	12 27	V			
				13 28	13 28				
				14 29	14 29	VI			
VI				15 30	15 30				
			Final Score:					Official Verification	

Subs: 1 2 3 4 5 6 7 8 9 10 11 12 13 14 15 16 17 18   Subs: 1 2 3 4 5 6 7 8 9 10 11 12 13 14 15 16 17 18

Comments: ....   Comments: ....

Referee: ....   Umpire: ....

Scorekeeper: ....

Key:

C=Playing Captain	1=Point	⊣ =Loss of Rally	□ =Point Scored Off Loss of Rally	△ =Libero Point
P-1=Penalty Point	P=Penalty	Px=Penalty Opponent	R=Reply	Rs=Re-Serve
T= Time-out	TX=Time-out Opponent	S=Substitution Serving Team	Sx=Opponent Substitution	

If the receiving team wins the rally, it receives a point which is recorded on the line of the NEXT server's
a number and a square is drawn around it. Also draw a square around the same point on the team's running score.

Date: Home: Visitor: Set #:

Time-Outs		Game No:				First Serve (Check Box Below)		Time-Outs			

| Serve Order | Player No | Team: | | | | | | | | | | | | | L: | | | | Serve Order | Player No | Team: | | | | | | | | | | | L: |

Serve Order	Player No	Team: L:	First Serve		Serve Order	Player No	Team: L:
I			1 16 / 2 17	1 16 / 2 17	I		
II			3 18 / 4 19 / 5 20	3 18 / 4 19 / 5 20	II		
III			6 21 / 7 22 / 8 23	6 21 / 7 22 / 8 23	III		
IV			9 24 / 10 25	9 24 / 10 25	IV		
V			11 26 / 12 27 / 13 28	11 26 / 12 27 / 13 28	V		
VI			14 29 / 15 30	14 29 / 15 30	VI		

Final Score: Official Verification

Subs: 1 2 3 4 5 6 7 8 9 10 11 12 13 14 15 16 17 18   Subs: 1 2 3 4 5 6 7 8 9 10 11 12 13 14 15 16 17 18

Comments: ....   Comments: ....

....

Referee: ....   Umpire: ....

Scorekeeper: ....

Key: C=Playing Captain   1=Point   ⊣ =Loss of Rally   ☐ =Point Scored Off Loss of Rally   △ =Libero Point

       P-1=Penalty Point   P=Penalty   Px=Penalty Opponent   R=Reply   Rs=Re-Serve

       T= Time-out   TX=Time-out Opponent   S=Substitution Serving Team   Sx=Opponent Substitution

If the receiving team wins the rally, it receives a point which is recorded on the line of the NEXT server's
a number and a square is drawn around it. Also draw a square around the same point on the team's running score.

Date: Home: Visitor: Set #:

Time-Outs		Game No:			First Serve (Check Box Below)		Time-Outs			
Serve Order	Player No	Team:	L:				Serve Order	Player No	Team:	L:
I					1 16 2 17	1 16 2 17	I			
II					3 18 4 19 5 20	3 18 4 19 5 20	II			
III					6 21 7 22	6 21 7 22	III			
IV					8 23 9 24 10 25	8 23 9 24 10 25	IV			
V					11 26 12 27 13 28	11 26 12 27 13 28	V			
VI					14 29 15 30	14 29 15 30	VI			
			Final Score:						Official Verification	

Subs: 1 2 3 4 5 6 7 8 9 10 11 12 13 14 15 16 17 18   Subs: 1 2 3 4 5 6 7 8 9 10 11 12 13 14 15 16 17 18

Comments: ....   Comments: ....

Referee: ....   Umpire: ....

Scorekeeper: ....

Key:

C=Playing Captain	1=Point	⊣ =Loss of Rally	☐ =Point Scored Off Loss of Rally	△ =Libero Point
P-1=Penalty Point	P=Penalty	Px=Penalty Opponent	R=Reply	Rs=Re-Serve
T= Time-out	TX=Time-out Opponent	S=Substitution Serving Team	Sx=Opponent Substitution	

If the receiving team wins the rally, it receives a point which is recorded on the line of the NEXT server's
a number and a square is drawn around it. Also draw a square around the same point on the team's running score.

Date: Home: Visitor: Set #:

Time-Outs		Game No:			First Serve (Check Box Below)		Time-Outs			

Serve Order	Player No	Team: L:								Serve Order	Player No	Team: L:							
I										1 16 1 16 2 17 2 17	I								
II										3 18 3 18 4 19 4 19 5 20 5 20	II								
III										6 21 6 21 7 22 7 22 8 23 8 23	III								
IV										9 24 9 24 10 25 10 25	IV								
V										11 26 11 26 12 27 12 27 13 28 13 28	V								
VI										14 29 14 29 15 30 15 30	VI								
		Final Score:											Official Verification						

Subs: 1 2 3 4 5 6 7 8 9 10 11 12 13 14 15 16 17 18   Subs: 1 2 3 4 5 6 7 8 9 10 11 12 13 14 15 16 17 18

Comments: ....   Comments: ....
....

Referee: ....   Umpire: ....

Scorekeeper: ....

Key:

C=Playing Captain	1=Point	⊣ =Loss of Rally	☐ =Point Scored Off Loss of Rally	△ =Libero Point
P-1=Penalty Point	P=Penalty	Px=Penalty Opponent	R=Reply	Rs=Re-Serve
T= Time-out	TX=Time-out Opponent	S=Substitution Serving Team	Sx=Opponent Substitution	

If the receiving team wins the rally, it receives a point which is recorded on the line of the NEXT server's
a number and a square is drawn around it. Also draw a square around the same point on the team's running score.

Date: Home: Visitor: Set #:

Time-Outs		Game No:			First Serve (Check Box Below)		Time-Outs			
Serve Order	Player No	Team:	L:				Serve Order	Player No	Team:	L:
I					1 16 / 2 17	1 16 / 2 17	I			
II					3 18 / 4 19 / 5 20	3 18 / 4 19 / 5 20	II			
III					6 21 / 7 22 / 8 23	6 21 / 7 22 / 8 23	III			
IV					9 24 / 10 25	9 24 / 10 25	IV			
V					11 26 / 12 27 / 13 28	11 26 / 12 27 / 13 28	V			
VI					14 29 / 15 30	14 29 / 15 30	VI			
			Final Score:							Official Verification

Subs: 1 2 3 4 5 6 7 8 9 10 11 12 13 14 15 16 17 18   Subs: 1 2 3 4 5 6 7 8 9 10 11 12 13 14 15 16 17 18

Comments: ....   Comments: ....

Referee: ....   Umpire: ....

Scorekeeper: ....

Key:
C=Playing Captain	1=Point	⊣ =Loss of Rally	☐ =Point Scored Off Loss of Rally	△ =Libero Point
P-1=Penalty Point	P=Penalty	Px=Penalty Opponent	R=Reply	Rs=Re-Serve
T= Time-out	TX=Time-out Opponent	S=Substitution Serving Team	Sx=Opponent Substitution	

If the receiving team wins the rally, it receives a point which is recorded on the line of the NEXT server's a number and a square is drawn around it. Also draw a square around the same point on the team's running score.

Date: Home: Visitor: Set #:

Time-Outs					First Serve (Check Box Below)		Time-Outs			
		Game No:								

Serve Order	Player No	Team:				L:			Serve Order	Player No	Team:			L:
I							1 16 / 2 17	1 16 / 2 17	I					
II							3 18 / 4 19 / 5 20	3 18 / 4 19 / 5 20	II					
III							6 21 / 7 22 / 8 23	6 21 / 7 22 / 8 23	III					
IV							9 24 / 10 25	9 24 / 10 25	IV					
V							11 26 / 12 27 / 13 28	11 26 / 12 27 / 13 28	V					
VI							14 29 / 15 30	14 29 / 15 30	VI					
					Final Score:								Official Verification	

Subs: 1 2 3 4 5 6 7 8 9 10 11 12 13 14 15 16 17 18   Subs: 1 2 3 4 5 6 7 8 9 10 11 12 13 14 15 16 17 18

Comments: ....   Comments: ....

Referee: ....   Umpire: ....

Scorekeeper: ....

Key:

C=Playing Captain	1=Point	⊣ =Loss of Rally	☐ =Point Scored Off Loss of Rally	△ =Libero Point
P-1=Penalty Point	P=Penalty	Px=Penalty Opponent	R=Reply	Rs=Re-Serve
T= Time-out	TX=Time-out Opponent	S=Substitution Serving Team	Sx=Opponent Substitution	

If the receiving team wins the rally, it receives a point which is recorded on the line of the NEXT server's
a number and a square is drawn around it. Also draw a square around the same point on the team's running score.

Date: _____ Home: _____ Visitor: _____ Set #: _____

Time-Outs		Game No:			First Serve (Check Box Below)		Time-Outs			

Serve Order	Player No	Team:			L:				Serve Order	Player No	Team:			L:

Serve Order		First Serve column 1	First Serve column 2	Serve Order
I		1 16 / 2 17	1 16 / 2 17	I
II		3 18 / 4 19 / 5 20	3 18 / 4 19 / 5 20	II
III		6 21 / 7 22	6 21 / 7 22	III
IV		8 23 / 9 24 / 10 25	8 23 / 9 24 / 10 25	IV
V		11 26 / 12 27 / 13 28	11 26 / 12 27 / 13 28	V
VI		14 29 / 15 30	14 29 / 15 30	VI

Final Score: _____   Official Verification _____

Subs: 1 2 3 4 5 6 7 8 9 10 11 12 13 14 15 16 17 18   Subs: 1 2 3 4 5 6 7 8 9 10 11 12 13 14 15 16 17 18

Comments: ....   Comments: ....

Referee: ....   Umpire: ....

Scorekeeper: ....

Key:

C=Playing Captain	1=Point	⊣ =Loss of Rally	☐ =Point Scored Off Loss of Rally	△ =Libero Point
P-1=Penalty Point	P=Penalty	Px=Penalty Opponent	R=Reply	Rs=Re-Serve
T= Time-out	TX=Time-out Opponent	S=Substitution Serving Team	Sx=Opponent Substitution	

If the receiving team wins the rally, it receives a point which is recorded on the line of the NEXT server's
a number and a square is drawn around it. Also draw a square around the same point on the team's running score.

Date: Home: Visitor: Set #:

Time-Outs		Game No:			First Serve (Check Box Below)		Time-Outs			

Serve Order	Player No	Team:				L:				Serve Order	Player No	Team:			L:

First Serve check boxes:

I	1 16 / 1 16	I
II	2 17 / 2 17	II
	3 18 / 3 18	
III	4 19 / 4 19	III
	5 20 / 5 20	
IV	6 21 / 6 21	IV
	7 22 / 7 22	
V	8 23 / 8 23	V
	9 24 / 9 24	
	10 25 / 10 25	
VI	11 26 / 11 26	VI
	12 27 / 12 27	
	13 28 / 13 28	
	14 29 / 14 29	
	15 30 / 15 30	

Final Score: Official Verification

Subs: 1 2 3 4 5 6 7 8 9 10 11 12 13 14 15 16 17 18   Subs: 1 2 3 4 5 6 7 8 9 10 11 12 13 14 15 16 17 18

Comments: ....   Comments: ....
....

Referee: ....   Umpire: ....

Scorekeeper: ....

Key:

C=Playing Captain	1=Point	⊣ =Loss of Rally	☐ =Point Scored Off Loss of Rally	△ =Libero Point
P-1=Penalty Point	P=Penalty	Px=Penalty Opponent	R=Reply	Rs=Re-Serve
T= Time-out	TX=Time-out Opponent	S=Substitution Serving Team	Sx=Opponent Substitution	

If the receiving team wins the rally, it receives a point which is recorded on the line of the NEXT server's
a number and a square is drawn around it. Also draw a square around the same point on the team's running score.

Date: Home: Visitor: Set #:

Time-Outs		Game No:			First Serve (Check Box Below)		Time-Outs			

Serve Order	Player No	Team:	L:				Serve Order	Player No	Team:	L:
I					1 16 2 17	1 16 2 17	I			
II					3 18 4 19 5 20	3 18 4 19 5 20	II			
III					6 21 7 22	6 21 7 22	III			
IV					8 23 9 24 10 25	8 23 9 24 10 25	IV			
V					11 26 12 27 13 28	11 26 12 27 13 28	V			
VI					14 29 15 30	14 29 15 30	VI			
			Final Score:						Official Verification	

Subs: 1 2 3 4 5 6 7 8 9 10 11 12 13 14 15 16 17 18   Subs: 1 2 3 4 5 6 7 8 9 10 11 12 13 14 15 16 17 18

Comments: ....   Comments: ....

Referee: ....   Umpire: ....

Scorekeeper: ....

Key:

C=Playing Captain	1=Point	⊣ =Loss of Rally	☐ =Point Scored Off Loss of Rally	△ =Libero Point
P-1=Penalty Point	P=Penalty	Px=Penalty Opponent	R=Reply	Rs=Re-Serve
T= Time-out	TX=Time-out Opponent	S=Substitution Serving Team	Sx=Opponent Substitution	

If the receiving team wins the rally, it receives a point which is recorded on the line of the NEXT server's
a number and a square is drawn around it. Also draw a square around the same point on the team's running score.

Date: Home: Visitor: Set #:

Time-Outs		Game No:			First Serve (Check Box Below)		Time-Outs			

Serve Order	Player No	Team:	L:				Serve Order	Player No	Team:	L:
I					1 16 2 17	1 16 2 17	I			
II					3 18 4 19 5 20	3 18 4 19 5 20	II			
III					6 21 7 22 8 23	6 21 7 22 8 23	III			
IV					9 24 10 25	9 24 10 25	IV			
V					11 26 12 27 13 28	11 26 12 27 13 28	V			
VI					14 29 15 30	14 29 15 30	VI			
			Final Score:						Official Verification	

Subs: 1 2 3 4 5 6 7 8 9 10 11 12 13 14 15 16 17 18   Subs: 1 2 3 4 5 6 7 8 9 10 11 12 13 14 15 16 17 18

Comments: ....   Comments: ....

Referee: ....   Umpire: ....

Scorekeeper: ....

Key:

C=Playing Captain	1=Point	⊣ =Loss of Rally	☐ =Point Scored Off Loss of Rally	△ =Libero Point
P-1=Penalty Point	P=Penalty	Px=Penalty Opponent	R=Reply	Rs=Re-Serve
T= Time-out	TX=Time-out Opponent	S=Substitution Serving Team	Sx=Opponent Substitution	

If the receiving team wins the rally, it receives a point which is recorded on the line of the NEXT server's
a number and a square is drawn around it. Also draw a square around the same point on the team's running score.

Date: Home: Visitor: Set #:

Time-Outs		Game No:			First Serve (Check Box Below)		Time-Outs			

Serve Order	Player No	Team:			L:				Serve Order	Player No	Team:			L:

Serve Order		First Serve columns		Serve Order
I		1 16 / 2 17	1 16 / 2 17	I
II		3 18 / 4 19 / 5 20	3 18 / 4 19 / 5 20	II
III		6 21 / 7 22	6 21 / 7 22	III
IV		8 23 / 9 24 / 10 25	8 23 / 9 24 / 10 25	IV
V		11 26 / 12 27 / 13 28	11 26 / 12 27 / 13 28	V
VI		14 29 / 15 30	14 29 / 15 30	VI

Final Score: Official Verification

Subs: 1 2 3 4 5 6 7 8 9 10 11 12 13 14 15 16 17 18   Subs: 1 2 3 4 5 6 7 8 9 10 11 12 13 14 15 16 17 18

Comments: ....   Comments: ....

Referee: ....   Umpire: ....

Scorekeeper: ....

Key:

C=Playing Captain	1=Point	⊣ =Loss of Rally	☐ =Point Scored Off Loss of Rally	△ =Libero Point
P-1=Penalty Point	P=Penalty	Px=Penalty Opponent	R=Reply	Rs=Re-Serve
T= Time-out	TX=Time-out Opponent	S=Substitution Serving Team	Sx=Opponent Substitution	

If the receiving team wins the rally, it receives a point which is recorded on the line of the NEXT server's
a number and a square is drawn around it. Also draw a square around the same point on the team's running score.

Date: Home: Visitor: Set #:

Time-Outs		Game No:		First Serve (Check Box Below)		Time-Outs			

Serve Order	Player No	Team:	L:			Serve Order	Player No	Team:	L:
I				1 16 2 17	1 16 2 17	I			
II				3 18 4 19 5 20	3 18 4 19 5 20	II			
III				6 21 7 22	6 21 7 22	III			
IV				8 23 9 24 10 25	8 23 9 24 10 25	IV			
V				11 26 12 27 13 28	11 26 12 27 13 28	V			
VI				14 29 15 30	14 29 15 30	VI			
			Final Score:						Official Verification

Subs: 1 2 3 4 5 6 7 8 9 10 11 12 13 14 15 16 17 18   Subs: 1 2 3 4 5 6 7 8 9 10 11 12 13 14 15 16 17 18

Comments: ....   Comments: ....

Referee: ....   Umpire: ....

Scorekeeper: ....

Key:
C=Playing Captain	1=Point	⊣ =Loss of Rally	☐ =Point Scored Off Loss of Rally	△ =Libero Point
P-1=Penalty Point	P=Penalty	Px=Penalty Opponent	R=Reply	Rs=Re-Serve
T= Time-out	TX=Time-out Opponent	S=Substitution Serving Team	Sx=Opponent Substitution	

If the receiving team wins the rally, it receives a point which is recorded on the line of the NEXT server's
a number and a square is drawn around it. Also draw a square around the same point on the team's running score.

Date: Home: Visitor: Set #:

Time-Outs			Game No:				First Serve (Check Box Below)		Time-Outs				

Serve Order	Player No	Team:				L:			Serve Order	Player No	Team:				L:

First Serve (Check Box Below):

1 16	1 16
2 17	2 17
3 18	3 18
4 19	4 19
5 20	5 20
6 21	6 21
7 22	7 22
8 23	8 23
9 24	9 24
10 25	10 25
11 26	11 26
12 27	12 27
13 28	13 28
14 29	14 29
15 30	15 30

Serve Order (Left team): I, II, III, IV, V, VI
Serve Order (Right team): I, II, III, IV, V, VI

Final Score: Official Verification

Subs: 1 2 3 4 5 6 7 8 9 10 11 12 13 14 15 16 17 18   Subs: 1 2 3 4 5 6 7 8 9 10 11 12 13 14 15 16 17 18

Comments: ....   Comments: ....

Referee: ....   Umpire: ....

Scorekeeper: ....

Key:

C=Playing Captain	1=Point	⊣ =Loss of Rally	☐ =Point Scored Off Loss of Rally	△ =Libero Point
P-1=Penalty Point	P=Penalty	Px=Penalty Opponent	R=Reply	Rs=Re-Serve
T= Time-out	TX=Time-out Opponent	S=Substitution Serving Team	Sx=Opponent Substitution	

If the receiving team wins the rally, it receives a point which is recorded on the line of the NEXT server's
a number and a square is drawn around it. Also draw a square around the same point on the team's running score.

Date: Home: Visitor: Set #:

Time-Outs		Game No:			First Serve (Check Box Below)		Time-Outs			
Serve Order	Player No	Team:	L:				Serve Order	Player No	Team:	L:
I					1 16	1 16	I			
					2 17	2 17				
II					3 18	3 18	II			
					4 19	4 19				
					5 20	5 20				
III					6 21	6 21	III			
					7 22	7 22				
IV					8 23	8 23	IV			
					9 24	9 24				
					10 25	10 25				
V					11 26	11 26	V			
					12 27	12 27				
					13 28	13 28				
VI					14 29	14 29	VI			
					15 30	15 30				
			Final Score:						Official Verification	

Subs: 1 2 3 4 5 6 7 8 9 10 11 12 13 14 15 16 17 18   Subs: 1 2 3 4 5 6 7 8 9 10 11 12 13 14 15 16 17 18

Comments: ....   Comments: ....

Referee: ....   Umpire: ....

Scorekeeper: ....

Key:
C=Playing Captain	1=Point	⊣ =Loss of Rally	☐ =Point Scored Off Loss of Rally	△ =Libero Point
P-1=Penalty Point	P=Penalty	Px=Penalty Opponent	R=Reply	Rs=Re-Serve
T= Time-out	TX=Time-out Opponent	S=Substitution Serving Team	Sx=Opponent Substitution	

If the receiving team wins the rally, it receives a point which is recorded on the line of the NEXT server's
a number and a square is drawn around it. Also draw a square around the same point on the team's running score.

Date: Home: Visitor: Set #:

Time-Outs		Game No:			First Serve (Check Box Below)		Time-Outs			

Serve Order	Player No	Team:					L:				Serve Order	Player No	Team:			L:

I											1 16	1 16	I								
II											2 17 / 3 18 / 4 19 / 5 20	2 17 / 3 18 / 4 19 / 5 20	II								
III											6 21 / 7 22	6 21 / 7 22	III								
IV											8 23 / 9 24 / 10 25	8 23 / 9 24 / 10 25	IV								
V											11 26 / 12 27 / 13 28	11 26 / 12 27 / 13 28	V								
VI											14 29 / 15 30	14 29 / 15 30	VI								

Final Score:

Official Verification

Subs: 1 2 3 4 5 6 7 8 9 10 11 12 13 14 15 16 17 18   Subs: 1 2 3 4 5 6 7 8 9 10 11 12 13 14 15 16 17 18

Comments: ....   Comments: ....
....

Referee: ....   Umpire: ....

Scorekeeper: ....

Key:

C=Playing Captain	1=Point	⊣ =Loss of Rally	☐ =Point Scored Off Loss of Rally	△ =Libero Point
P-1=Penalty Point	P=Penalty	Px=Penalty Opponent	R=Reply	Rs=Re-Serve
T= Time-out	TX=Time-out Opponent	S=Substitution Serving Team	Sx=Opponent Substitution	

If the receiving team wins the rally, it receives a point which is recorded on the line of the NEXT server's
a number and a square is drawn around it. Also draw a square around the same point on the team's running score.

Date: Home: Visitor: Set #:

Time-Outs		Game No:			First Serve (Check Box Below)		Time-Outs			

Serve Order	Player No	Team:	L:				Serve Order	Player No	Team:	L:
I					1 16	1 16	I			
					2 17	2 17				
II					3 18	3 18	II			
					4 19	4 19				
					5 20	5 20				
III					6 21	6 21	III			
					7 22	7 22				
					8 23	8 23				
IV					9 24	9 24	IV			
					10 25	10 25				
V					11 26	11 26	V			
					12 27	12 27				
					13 28	13 28				
VI					14 29	14 29	VI			
					15 30	15 30				
			Final Score:						Official Verification	

Subs: **1 2 3 4 5 6 7 8 9 10 11 12 13 14 15 16 17 18**   Subs: **1 2 3 4 5 6 7 8 9 10 11 12 13 14 15 16 17 18**

Comments: ....   Comments: ....

Referee: ....   Umpire: ....

Scorekeeper: ....

Key:

C=Playing Captain	1=Point	⊣ =Loss of Rally	☐ =Point Scored Off Loss of Rally	△ =Libero Point
P-1=Penalty Point	P=Penalty	Px=Penalty Opponent	R=Reply	Rs=Re-Serve
T= Time-out	TX=Time-out Opponent	S=Substitution Serving Team	Sx=Opponent Substitution	

If the receiving team wins the rally, it receives a point which is recorded on the line of the NEXT server's
a number and a square is drawn around it. Also draw a square around the same point on the team's running score.

Date: Home: Visitor: Set #:

Time-Outs		Game No:			First Serve (Check Box Below)		Time-Outs			

Serve Order	Player No	Team:	L:				Serve Order	Player No	Team:	L:
I					1 16	1 16	I			
					2 17	2 17				
II					3 18	3 18	II			
					4 19	4 19				
					5 20	5 20				
III					6 21	6 21	III			
					7 22	7 22				
					8 23	8 23				
IV					9 24	9 24	IV			
					10 25	10 25				
V					11 26	11 26	V			
					12 27	12 27				
					13 28	13 28				
VI					14 29	14 29	VI			
					15 30	15 30				
			Final Score:						Official Verification	

Subs: 1 2 3 4 5 6 7 8 9 10 11 12 13 14 15 16 17 18   Subs: 1 2 3 4 5 6 7 8 9 10 11 12 13 14 15 16 17 18

Comments: ....   Comments: ....

Referee: ....   Umpire: ....

Scorekeeper: ....

Key:
- C=Playing Captain
- 1=Point
- ⊣ =Loss of Rally
- ☐ =Point Scored Off Loss of Rally
- △ =Libero Point
- P-1=Penalty Point
- P=Penalty
- Px=Penalty Opponent
- R=Reply
- Rs=Re-Serve
- T= Time-out
- TX=Time-out Opponent
- S=Substitution Serving Team
- Sx=Opponent Substitution

If the receiving team wins the rally, it receives a point which is recorded on the line of the NEXT server's
a number and a square is drawn around it. Also draw a square around the same point on the team's running score.

Date: Home: Visitor: Set #:

Time-Outs		Game No:				First Serve (Check Box Below)		Time-Outs			
Serve Order	Player No	Team:		L:				Serve Order	Player No	Team:	L:
I						1 16 2 17	1 16 2 17	I			
II						3 18 4 19 5 20	3 18 4 19 5 20	II			
III						6 21 7 22	6 21 7 22	III			
IV						8 23 9 24 10 25	8 23 9 24 10 25	IV			
V						11 26 12 27 13 28	11 26 12 27 13 28	V			
VI						14 29 15 30	14 29 15 30	VI			
				Final Score:						Official Verification	

Subs: 1 2 3 4 5 6 7 8 9 10 11 12 13 14 15 16 17 18   Subs: 1 2 3 4 5 6 7 8 9 10 11 12 13 14 15 16 17 18

Comments: ....   Comments: ....

....

Referee: ....   Umpire: ....

Scorekeeper: ....

Key:

C=Playing Captain	1=Point	⊣ =Loss of Rally	☐ =Point Scored Off Loss of Rally	△ =Libero Point
P-1=Penalty Point	P=Penalty	Px=Penalty Opponent	R=Reply	Rs=Re-Serve
T= Time-out	TX=Time-out Opponent	S=Substitution Serving Team	Sx=Opponent Substitution	

If the receiving team wins the rally, it receives a point which is recorded on the line of the NEXT server's
a number and a square is drawn around it. Also draw a square around the same point on the team's running score.

Date: Home: Visitor: Set #:

Time-Outs		Game No:				First Serve (Check Box Below)		Time-Outs			

Serve Order	Player No	Team: L:						Serve Order	Player No	Team: L:	
I						1 16 2 17	1 16 2 17	I			
II						3 18 4 19 5 20	3 18 4 19 5 20	II			
III						6 21 7 22	6 21 7 22	III			
IV						8 23 9 24 10 25	8 23 9 24 10 25	IV			
V						11 26 12 27 13 28	11 26 12 27 13 28	V			
VI						14 29 15 30	14 29 15 30	VI			
				Final Score:						Official Verification	

Subs: 1 2 3 4 5 6 7 8 9 10 11 12 13 14 15 16 17 18   Subs: 1 2 3 4 5 6 7 8 9 10 11 12 13 14 15 16 17 18

Comments: ....   Comments: ....

Referee: ....   Umpire: ....

Scorekeeper: ....

Key:

C=Playing Captain	1=Point	⊣ =Loss of Rally	☐ =Point Scored Off Loss of Rally	△ =Libero Point
P-1=Penalty Point	P=Penalty	Px=Penalty Opponent	R=Reply	Rs=Re-Serve
T= Time-out	TX=Time-out Opponent	S=Substitution Serving Team	Sx=Opponent Substitution	

If the receiving team wins the rally, it receives a point which is recorded on the line of the NEXT server's
a number and a square is drawn around it. Also draw a square around the same point on the team's running score.

Date: Home: Visitor: Set #:

Time-Outs		Game No:			First Serve (Check Box Below)		Time-Outs			

Serve Order	Player No	Team:		L:			Serve Order	Player No	Team:		L:
I					1 16 2 17	1 16 2 17	I				
II					3 18 4 19 5 20	3 18 4 19 5 20	II				
III					6 21 7 22	6 21 7 22	III				
IV					8 23 9 24 10 25	8 23 9 24 10 25	IV				
V					11 26 12 27 13 28	11 26 12 27 13 28	V				
VI					14 29 15 30	14 29 15 30	VI				
			Final Score:							Official Verification	

Subs: 1 2 3 4 5 6 7 8 9 10 11 12 13 14 15 16 17 18   Subs: 1 2 3 4 5 6 7 8 9 10 11 12 13 14 15 16 17 18

Comments: ....   Comments: ....

....

Referee: ....   Umpire: ....

Scorekeeper: ....

Key:

C=Playing Captain	1=Point	⊣ =Loss of Rally	☐ =Point Scored Off Loss of Rally	△ =Libero Point
P-1=Penalty Point	P=Penalty	Px=Penalty Opponent	R=Reply	Rs=Re-Serve
T= Time-out	TX=Time-out Opponent	S=Substitution Serving Team	Sx=Opponent Substitution	

If the receiving team wins the rally, it receives a point which is recorded on the line of the NEXT server's
a number and a square is drawn around it. Also draw a square around the same point on the team's running score.

Date:　　　　　Home:　　　　　Visitor:　　　　　Set #:

Time-Outs		Game No:			First Serve (Check Box Below)		Time-Outs			
Serve Order	Player No	Team:	L:				Serve Order	Player No	Team:	L:
I					1 16 2 17	1 16 2 17	I			
II					3 18 4 19 5 20	3 18 4 19 5 20	II			
III					6 21 7 22 8 23	6 21 7 22 8 23	III			
IV					9 24 10 25	9 24 10 25	IV			
V					11 26 12 27 13 28	11 26 12 27 13 28	V			
VI					14 29 15 30	14 29 15 30	VI			
			Final Score:						Official Verification	

Subs: 1 2 3 4 5 6 7 8 9 10 11 12 13 14 15 16 17 18　　　　Subs: 1 2 3 4 5 6 7 8 9 10 11 12 13 14 15 16 17 18

Comments: ....　　Comments: ....

Referee: ....　　Umpire: ....

Scorekeeper: ....

Key:
C=Playing Captain	1=Point	⊣ =Loss of Rally	☐ =Point Scored Off Loss of Rally	△ =Libero Point
P-1=Penalty Point	P=Penalty	Px=Penalty Opponent	R=Reply	Rs=Re-Serve
T= Time-out	TX=Time-out Opponent	S=Substitution Serving Team	Sx=Opponent Substitution	

If the receiving team wins the rally, it receives a point which is recorded on the line of the NEXT server's
a number and a square is drawn around it. Also draw a square around the same point on the team's running score.

Date:　　　　　　　Home:　　　　　　　　Visitor:　　　　　　　　Set #:

Time-Outs		Game No:				First Serve (Check Box Below)		Time-Outs			
Serve Order	Player No	Team:　　　　　　　　　L:						Serve Order	Player No	Team:　　　　　　L:	
I						1 16 / 2 17	1 16 / 2 17	I			
II						3 18 / 4 19 / 5 20	3 18 / 4 19 / 5 20	II			
III						6 21 / 7 22	6 21 / 7 22	III			
IV						8 23 / 9 24 / 10 25	8 23 / 9 24 / 10 25	IV			
V						11 26 / 12 27 / 13 28	11 26 / 12 27 / 13 28	V			
VI						14 29 / 15 30	14 29 / 15 30	VI			
		Final Score:								Official Verification	

Subs: 1 2 3 4 5 6 7 8 9 10 11 12 13 14 15 16 17 18　　　　　Subs: 1 2 3 4 5 6 7 8 9 10 11 12 13 14 15 16 17 18

Comments: ....　　Comments: ....
....

Referee: ....　　Umpire: ....

Scorekeeper: ....

Key:

C=Playing Captain	1=Point	⊣ =Loss of Rally	☐ =Point Scored Off Loss of Rally	△ =Libero Point
P-1=Penalty Point	P=Penalty	Px=Penalty Opponent	R=Reply	Rs=Re-Serve
T= Time-out	TX=Time-out Opponent	S=Substitution Serving Team	Sx=Opponent Substitution	

If the receiving team wins the rally, it receives a point which is recorded on the line of the NEXT server's
a number and a square is drawn around it. Also draw a square around the same point on the team's running score.

Date: Home: Visitor: Set #:

Time-Outs		Game No:			First Serve (Check Box Below)		Time-Outs			

Serve Order	Player No	Team:					L:													Serve Order	Player No	Team:				L:												
I																1 16 / 2 17	1 16 / 2 17	I																	
II																3 18 / 4 19 / 5 20	3 18 / 4 19 / 5 20	II																	
III																6 21 / 7 22	6 21 / 7 22	III																	
IV																8 23 / 9 24 / 10 25	8 23 / 9 24 / 10 25	IV																	
V																11 26 / 12 27 / 13 28	11 26 / 12 27 / 13 28	V																	
VI																14 29 / 15 30	14 29 / 15 30	VI																	

Final Score: | | | Official Verification

Subs: 1 2 3 4 5 6 7 8 9 10 11 12 13 14 15 16 17 18   Subs: 1 2 3 4 5 6 7 8 9 10 11 12 13 14 15 16 17 18

Comments: ....   Comments: ....

Referee: ....   Umpire: ....

Scorekeeper: ....

Key:

C=Playing Captain	1=Point	⊣ =Loss of Rally	☐ =Point Scored Off Loss of Rally	△ =Libero Point
P-1=Penalty Point	P=Penalty	Px=Penalty Opponent	R=Reply	Rs=Re-Serve
T= Time-out	TX=Time-out Opponent	S=Substitution Serving Team	Sx=Opponent Substitution	

If the receiving team wins the rally, it receives a point which is recorded on the line of the NEXT server's
a number and a square is drawn around it. Also draw a square around the same point on the team's running score.

Date: Home: Visitor: Set #:

Time-Outs		Game No:			First Serve (Check Box Below)		Time-Outs			

Serve Order	Player No	Team:			L:			Serve Order	Player No	Team:			L:
I						1 16 / 2 17	1 16 / 2 17	I					
II						3 18 / 4 19 / 5 20	3 18 / 4 19 / 5 20	II					
III						6 21 / 7 22	6 21 / 7 22	III					
IV						8 23 / 9 24 / 10 25	8 23 / 9 24 / 10 25	IV					
V						11 26 / 12 27 / 13 28	11 26 / 12 27 / 13 28	V					
VI						14 29 / 15 30	14 29 / 15 30	VI					

Final Score: Official Verification

Subs: 1 2 3 4 5 6 7 8 9 10 11 12 13 14 15 16 17 18   Subs: 1 2 3 4 5 6 7 8 9 10 11 12 13 14 15 16 17 18

Comments: ....   Comments: ....

Referee: ....   Umpire: ....

Scorekeeper: ....

Key:

C=Playing Captain	1=Point	⊣ =Loss of Rally	☐ =Point Scored Off Loss of Rally	△ =Libero Point
P-1=Penalty Point	P=Penalty	Px=Penalty Opponent	R=Reply	Rs=Re-Serve
T= Time-out	TX=Time-out Opponent	S=Substitution Serving Team	Sx=Opponent Substitution	

If the receiving team wins the rally, it receives a point which is recorded on the line of the NEXT server's
a number and a square is drawn around it. Also draw a square around the same point on the team's running score.

Date: Home: Visitor: Set #:

Time-Outs		Game No:					First Serve (Check Box Below)		Time-Outs			

| Serve Order | Player No | Team: | | | | | | L: | | | | | | | | | | | Serve Order | Player No | Team: | | | | | | L: | | | | | | | |

Serve Order							First Serve col 1	First Serve col 2	Serve Order	
I							1 16 / 2 17	1 16 / 2 17	I	
II							3 18 / 4 19 / 5 20	3 18 / 4 19 / 5 20	II	
III							6 21 / 7 22	6 21 / 7 22	III	
IV							8 23 / 9 24 / 10 25	8 23 / 9 24 / 10 25	IV	
V							11 26 / 12 27 / 13 28	11 26 / 12 27 / 13 28	V	
VI							14 29 / 15 30	14 29 / 15 30	VI	

Final Score:

Official Verification

Subs: 1 2 3 4 5 6 7 8 9 10 11 12 13 14 15 16 17 18

Subs: 1 2 3 4 5 6 7 8 9 10 11 12 13 14 15 16 17 18

Comments: ....

Comments: ....

Referee: ....

Umpire: ....

Scorekeeper: ....

Key:

C=Playing Captain	1=Point	⊣ =Loss of Rally	☐ =Point Scored Off Loss of Rally	△ =Libero Point
P-1=Penalty Point	P=Penalty	Px=Penalty Opponent	R=Reply	Rs=Re-Serve
T= Time-out	TX=Time-out Opponent	S=Substitution Serving Team	Sx=Opponent Substitution	

If the receiving team wins the rally, it receives a point which is recorded on the line of the NEXT server's
a number and a square is drawn around it. Also draw a square around the same point on the team's running score.

Date: Home: Visitor: Set #:

Time-Outs		Game No:			First Serve (Check Box Below)		Time-Outs			
Serve Order	**Player No**	**Team:**	**L:**				**Serve Order**	**Player No**	**Team:**	**L:**
I					1 16 2 17	1 16 2 17	I			
II					3 18 4 19 5 20	3 18 4 19 5 20	II			
III					6 21 7 22	6 21 7 22	III			
IV					8 23 9 24 10 25	8 23 9 24 10 25	IV			
V					11 26 12 27 13 28	11 26 12 27 13 28	V			
VI					14 29 15 30	14 29 15 30	VI			
			Final Score:						**Official Verification**	

Subs: 1 2 3 4 5 6 7 8 9 10 11 12 13 14 15 16 17 18   Subs: 1 2 3 4 5 6 7 8 9 10 11 12 13 14 15 16 17 18

Comments: ....   Comments: ....

Referee: Umpire:

Scorekeeper:

Key:

C=Playing Captain	1=Point	⊣ =Loss of Rally	☐ =Point Scored Off Loss of Rally	△ =Libero Point
P-1=Penalty Point	P=Penalty	Px=Penalty Opponent	R=Reply	Rs=Re-Serve
T= Time-out	TX=Time-out Opponent	S=Substitution Serving Team	Sx=Opponent Substitution	

If the receiving team wins the rally, it receives a point which is recorded on the line of the NEXT server's
a number and a square is drawn around it. Also draw a square around the same point on the team's running score.

Date: Home: Visitor: Set #:

Time-Outs		Game No:						First Serve (Check Box Below)		Time-Outs			

Serve Order	Player No	Team:						L:									Serve Order	Player No	Team:						L:

First Serve point columns:

1 16	1 16
2 17	2 17
3 18	3 18
4 19	4 19
5 20	5 20
6 21	6 21
7 22	7 22
8 23	8 23
9 24	9 24
10 25	10 25
11 26	11 26
12 27	12 27
13 28	13 28
14 29	14 29
15 30	15 30

Serve Order rows (both sides): I, II, III, IV, V, VI

Final Score: Official Verification

Subs: 1 2 3 4 5 6 7 8 9 10 11 12 13 14 15 16 17 18   Subs: 1 2 3 4 5 6 7 8 9 10 11 12 13 14 15 16 17 18

Comments: ....   Comments: ....

Referee: ....   Umpire: ....

Scorekeeper: ....

Key:

C=Playing Captain	1=Point	⊣ =Loss of Rally	☐ =Point Scored Off Loss of Rally	△ =Libero Point
P-1=Penalty Point	P=Penalty	Px=Penalty Opponent	R=Reply	Rs=Re-Serve
T= Time-out	TX=Time-out Opponent	S=Substitution Serving Team	Sx=Opponent Substitution	

If the receiving team wins the rally, it receives a point which is recorded on the line of the NEXT server's
a number and a square is drawn around it. Also draw a square around the same point on the team's running score.

Date: Home: Visitor: Set #:

Time-Outs		Game No:			First Serve (Check Box Below)			Time-Outs			
Serve Order	Player No	Team:		L:			Serve Order	Player No	Team:		L:
I					1 16	1 16	I				
					2 17	2 17					
II					3 18	3 18	II				
					4 19	4 19					
					5 20	5 20					
III					6 21	6 21	III				
					7 22	7 22					
IV					8 23	8 23	IV				
					9 24	9 24					
					10 25	10 25					
V					11 26	11 26	V				
					12 27	12 27					
					13 28	13 28					
VI					14 29	14 29	VI				
					15 30	15 30					
				Final Score:						Official Verification	

Subs: 1 2 3 4 5 6 7 8 9 10 11 12 13 14 15 16 17 18   Subs: 1 2 3 4 5 6 7 8 9 10 11 12 13 14 15 16 17 18

Comments: ....   Comments: ....

Referee: ....   Umpire: ....

Scorekeeper: ....

Key:

C=Playing Captain	1=Point	⊣ =Loss of Rally	☐ =Point Scored Off Loss of Rally	△ =Libero Point
P-1=Penalty Point	P=Penalty	Px=Penalty Opponent	R=Reply	Rs=Re-Serve
T= Time-out	TX=Time-out Opponent	S=Substitution Serving Team	Sx=Opponent Substitution	

If the receiving team wins the rally, it receives a point which is recorded on the line of the NEXT server's
a number and a square is drawn around it. Also draw a square around the same point on the team's running score.

Date: _____ Home: _____ Visitor: _____ Set #: _____

Time-Outs		Game No:			First Serve (Check Box Below)		Time-Outs			

Serve Order	Player No	Team:	L:				Serve Order	Player No	Team:	L:
I					1 16 2 17	1 16 2 17	I			
II					3 18 4 19 5 20	3 18 4 19 5 20	II			
III					6 21 7 22	6 21 7 22	III			
IV					8 23 9 24 10 25	8 23 9 24 10 25	IV			
V					11 26 12 27 13 28	11 26 12 27 13 28	V			
VI					14 29 15 30	14 29 15 30	VI			
			Final Score:						Official Verification	

Subs: 1 2 3 4 5 6 7 8 9 10 11 12 13 14 15 16 17 18   Subs: 1 2 3 4 5 6 7 8 9 10 11 12 13 14 15 16 17 18

Comments: ....   Comments: ....

Referee: ....   Umpire: ....

Scorekeeper: ....

Key:

C=Playing Captain	1=Point	⊣ =Loss of Rally	☐ =Point Scored Off Loss of Rally	△ =Libero Point
P-1=Penalty Point	P=Penalty	Px=Penalty Opponent	R=Reply	Rs=Re-Serve
T= Time-out	TX=Time-out Opponent	S=Substitution Serving Team	Sx=Opponent Substitution	

If the receiving team wins the rally, it receives a point which is recorded on the line of the NEXT server's
a number and a square is drawn around it. Also draw a square around the same point on the team's running score.

Date: Home: Visitor: Set #:

Time-Outs		Game No:				First Serve (Check Box Below)		Time-Outs			

Serve Order	Player No	Team: L:					Serve Order	Player No	Team: L:		
I				1 16	1 16	I					
				2 17	2 17						
II				3 18	3 18	II					
				4 19	4 19						
				5 20	5 20						
III				6 21	6 21	III					
				7 22	7 22						
				8 23	8 23						
IV				9 24	9 24	IV					
				10 25	10 25						
V				11 26	11 26	V					
				12 27	12 27						
				13 28	13 28						
VI				14 29	14 29	VI					
				15 30	15 30						

Final Score:		Official Verification	

Subs: 1 2 3 4 5 6 7 8 9 10 11 12 13 14 15 16 17 18   Subs: 1 2 3 4 5 6 7 8 9 10 11 12 13 14 15 16 17 18

Comments: ....   Comments: ....

Referee: ....   Umpire: ....

Scorekeeper: ....

Key:

C=Playing Captain	1=Point	⊣ =Loss of Rally	☐ =Point Scored Off Loss of Rally	△ =Libero Point
P-1=Penalty Point	P=Penalty	Px=Penalty Opponent	R=Reply	Rs=Re-Serve
T= Time-out	TX=Time-out Opponent	S=Substitution Serving Team	Sx=Opponent Substitution	

If the receiving team wins the rally, it receives a point which is recorded on the line of the NEXT server's
a number and a square is drawn around it. Also draw a square around the same point on the team's running score.

Date:　　　　　　Home:　　　　　　Visitor:　　　　　　Set #:

Time-Outs		Game No:		First Serve (Check Box Below)		Time-Outs			

Serve Order	Player No	Team:			L:			Serve Order	Player No	Team:			L:

Serve Order																	
I			1 16	1 16	I
			2 17	2 17	
II			3 18	3 18	II
			4 19	4 19	
			5 20	5 20	
III			6 21	6 21	III
			7 22	7 22	
			8 23	8 23	
IV			9 24	9 24	IV
			10 25	10 25	
V			11 26	11 26	V
			12 27	12 27	
			13 28	13 28	
VI			14 29	14 29	VI
			15 30	15 30	

Final Score:　　　　　　Official Verification

Subs: 1 2 3 4 5 6 7 8 9 10 11 12 13 14 15 16 17 18　　　　Subs: 1 2 3 4 5 6 7 8 9 10 11 12 13 14 15 16 17 18

Comments: ....　Comments: ....

Referee: ....　Umpire: ....

Scorekeeper: ....

Key:

C=Playing Captain	1=Point	⊣ =Loss of Rally	☐ =Point Scored Off Loss of Rally	△ =Libero Point
P-1=Penalty Point	P=Penalty	Px=Penalty Opponent	R=Reply	Rs=Re-Serve
T= Time-out	TX=Time-out Opponent	S=Substitution Serving Team	Sx=Opponent Substitution	

If the receiving team wins the rally, it receives a point which is recorded on the line of the NEXT server's
a number and a square is drawn around it. Also draw a square around the same point on the team's running score.

Date: Home: Visitor: Set #:

Time-Outs		Game No:			First Serve (Check Box Below)		Time-Outs			

Serve Order	Player No	Team:	L:				Serve Order	Player No	Team:	L:
I				1 16	1 16		I			
				2 17	2 17					
II				3 18	3 18		II			
				4 19	4 19					
				5 20	5 20					
III				6 21	6 21		III			
				7 22	7 22					
				8 23	8 23					
IV				9 24	9 24		IV			
				10 25	10 25					
V				11 26	11 26		V			
				12 27	12 27					
				13 28	13 28					
VI				14 29	14 29		VI			
				15 30	15 30					
		Final Score:							Official Verification	

Subs: 1 2 3 4 5 6 7 8 9 10 11 12 13 14 15 16 17 18

Subs: 1 2 3 4 5 6 7 8 9 10 11 12 13 14 15 16 17 18

Comments: ....

Comments: ....

Referee: ....

Umpire: ....

Scorekeeper: ....

Key:

C=Playing Captain	1=Point	⊣ =Loss of Rally	☐ =Point Scored Off Loss of Rally	△ =Libero Point
P-1=Penalty Point	P=Penalty	Px=Penalty Opponent	R=Reply	Rs=Re-Serve
T= Time-out	TX=Time-out Opponent	S=Substitution Serving Team	Sx=Opponent Substitution	

If the receiving team wins the rally, it receives a point which is recorded on the line of the NEXT server's
a number and a square is drawn around it. Also draw a square around the same point on the team's running score.

Date: Home: Visitor: Set #:

Time-Outs		Game No:			First Serve (Check Box Below)		Time-Outs			
Serve Order	Player No	Team:	L:				Serve Order	Player No	Team:	L:
I					1 16 2 17	1 16 2 17	I			
II					3 18 4 19 5 20	3 18 4 19 5 20	II			
III					6 21 7 22	6 21 7 22	III			
IV					8 23 9 24 10 25	8 23 9 24 10 25	IV			
V					11 26 12 27 13 28	11 26 12 27 13 28	V			
VI					14 29 15 30	14 29 15 30	VI			
			Final Score:						Official Verification	

Subs: **1 2 3 4 5 6 7 8 9 10 11 12 13 14 15 16 17 18**   Subs: **1 2 3 4 5 6 7 8 9 10 11 12 13 14 15 16 17 18**

Comments: ....   Comments: ....

Referee: ....   Umpire: ....

Scorekeeper: ....

Key:

C=Playing Captain	1=Point	⊣ =Loss of Rally	☐ =Point Scored Off Loss of Rally	△ =Libero Point
P-1=Penalty Point	P=Penalty	Px=Penalty Opponent	R=Reply	Rs=Re-Serve
T= Time-out	TX=Time-out Opponent	S=Substitution Serving Team	Sx=Opponent Substitution	

If the receiving team wins the rally, it receives a point which is recorded on the line of the NEXT server's
a number and a square is drawn around it. Also draw a square around the same point on the team's running score.

Date: Home: Visitor: Set #:

	Time-Outs		Game No:			First Serve (Check Box Below)			Time-Outs			
Serve Order	Player No	Team:		L:				Serve Order	Player No	Team:		L:
I						1 16	1 16	I				
						2 17	2 17					
II						3 18	3 18	II				
						4 19	4 19					
						5 20	5 20					
III						6 21	6 21	III				
						7 22	7 22					
						8 23	8 23					
IV						9 24	9 24	IV				
						10 25	10 25					
V						11 26	11 26	V				
						12 27	12 27					
						13 28	13 28					
VI						14 29	14 29	VI				
						15 30	15 30					
				Final Score:							Official Verification	

Subs: 1 2 3 4 5 6 7 8 9 10 11 12 13 14 15 16 17 18   Subs: 1 2 3 4 5 6 7 8 9 10 11 12 13 14 15 16 17 18

Comments: ....   Comments: ....

Referee: ....   Umpire: ....

Scorekeeper: ....

Key:

C=Playing Captain	1=Point	⊣ =Loss of Rally	☐ =Point Scored Off Loss of Rally	△ =Libero Point
P-1=Penalty Point	P=Penalty	Px=Penalty Opponent	R=Reply	Rs=Re-Serve
T= Time-out	TX=Time-out Opponent	S=Substitution Serving Team	Sx=Opponent Substitution	

If the receiving team wins the rally, it receives a point which is recorded on the line of the NEXT server's
a number and a square is drawn around it. Also draw a square around the same point on the team's running score.

Date:	Home:	Visitor:	Set #:

Time-Outs		Game No:			First Serve (Check Box Below)		Time-Outs			

| Serve Order | Player No | Team: | | | | | | | | L: | | | | | | | | | | Serve Order | Player No | Team: | | | | | | | | L: |

Serve Order	Player No	Team: L:		Serve Order	Player No	Team: L:
I			1 16 / 2 17	1 16 / 2 17	I	
II			3 18 / 4 19 / 5 20	3 18 / 4 19 / 5 20	II	
III			6 21 / 7 22	6 21 / 7 22	III	
IV			8 23 / 9 24 / 10 25	8 23 / 9 24 / 10 25	IV	
V			11 26 / 12 27 / 13 28	11 26 / 12 27 / 13 28	V	
VI			14 29 / 15 30	14 29 / 15 30	VI	

Final Score:			Official Verification	

Subs: 1 2 3 4 5 6 7 8 9 10 11 12 13 14 15 16 17 18   Subs: 1 2 3 4 5 6 7 8 9 10 11 12 13 14 15 16 17 18

Comments: ....   Comments: ....

Referee: ....   Umpire: ....

Scorekeeper: ....

Key:
C=Playing Captain	1=Point	⊣ =Loss of Rally	☐ =Point Scored Off Loss of Rally	△ =Libero Point
P-1=Penalty Point	P=Penalty	Px=Penalty Opponent	R=Reply	Rs=Re-Serve
T= Time-out	TX=Time-out Opponent	S=Substitution Serving Team	Sx=Opponent Substitution	

If the receiving team wins the rally, it receives a point which is recorded on the line of the NEXT server's
a number and a square is drawn around it. Also draw a square around the same point on the team's running score.

Date: Home: Visitor: Set #:

Time-Outs		Game No:				First Serve (Check Box Below)		Time-Outs			
Serve Order	Player No	**Team:**		L:				Serve Order	Player No	**Team:**	L:
I						1 16 2 17	1 16 2 17	I			
II						3 18 4 19 5 20	3 18 4 19 5 20	II			
III						6 21 7 22	6 21 7 22	III			
IV						8 23 9 24 10 25	8 23 9 24 10 25	IV			
V						11 26 12 27 13 28	11 26 12 27 13 28	V			
VI						14 29 15 30	14 29 15 30	VI			
			Final Score:							Official Verification	

Subs: **1 2 3 4 5 6 7 8 9 10 11 12 13 14 15 16 17 18**   Subs: **1 2 3 4 5 6 7 8 9 10 11 12 13 14 15 16 17 18**

Comments: ....   Comments: ....

Referee: ....   Umpire: ....

Scorekeeper: ....

Key: C=Playing Captain   1=Point   ⊣ =Loss of Rally   ☐ =Point Scored Off Loss of Rally   △ =Libero Point

       P-1=Penalty Point   P=Penalty   Px=Penalty Opponent   R=Reply   Rs=Re-Serve

       T= Time-out   TX=Time-out Opponent   S=Substitution Serving Team   Sx=Opponent Substitution

If the receiving team wins the rally, it receives a point which is recorded on the line of the NEXT server's
a number and a square is drawn around it. Also draw a square around the same point on the team's running score.

Date:	Home:	Visitor:	Set #:

Time-Outs		Game No:		First Serve (Check Box Below)		Time-Outs			

Serve Order	Player No	Team:	L:			Serve Order	Player No	Team:	L:
I				1 16	1 16	I			
				2 17	2 17				
II				3 18	3 18	II			
				4 19	4 19				
				5 20	5 20				
III				6 21	6 21	III			
				7 22	7 22				
				8 23	8 23				
IV				9 24	9 24	IV			
				10 25	10 25				
V				11 26	11 26	V			
				12 27	12 27				
				13 28	13 28				
VI				14 29	14 29	VI			
				15 30	15 30				

Final Score: Official Verification

Subs: 1 2 3 4 5 6 7 8 9 10 11 12 13 14 15 16 17 18   Subs: 1 2 3 4 5 6 7 8 9 10 11 12 13 14 15 16 17 18

Comments: ....   Comments: ....
....

Referee: ....   Umpire: ....

Scorekeeper: ....

Key:
C=Playing Captain	1=Point	⊣ =Loss of Rally	□ =Point Scored Off Loss of Rally	△ =Libero Point
P-1=Penalty Point	P=Penalty	Px=Penalty Opponent	R=Reply	Rs=Re-Serve
T= Time-out	TX=Time-out Opponent	S=Substitution Serving Team	Sx=Opponent Substitution	

If the receiving team wins the rally, it receives a point which is recorded on the line of the NEXT server's
a number and a square is drawn around it. Also draw a square around the same point on the team's running score.

Date: Home: Visitor: Set #:

	Time-Outs		Game No:			First Serve (Check Box Below)		Time-Outs			
Serve Order	Player No	Team:		L:				Serve Order	Player No	Team:	L:
I						1 16 2 17	1 16 2 17	I			
II						3 18 4 19 5 20	3 18 4 19 5 20	II			
III						6 21 7 22	6 21 7 22	III			
IV						8 23 9 24 10 25	8 23 9 24 10 25	IV			
V						11 26 12 27 13 28	11 26 12 27 13 28	V			
VI						14 29 15 30	14 29 15 30	VI			
				Final Score:						Official Verification	

Subs: 1 2 3 4 5 6 7 8 9 10 11 12 13 14 15 16 17 18   Subs: 1 2 3 4 5 6 7 8 9 10 11 12 13 14 15 16 17 18

Comments: ....   Comments: ....
....

Referee: ....   Umpire: ....

Scorekeeper: ....

Key:

C=Playing Captain	1=Point	⊣ =Loss of Rally	☐ =Point Scored Off Loss of Rally	△ =Libero Point
P-1=Penalty Point	P=Penalty	Px=Penalty Opponent	R=Reply	Rs=Re-Serve
T= Time-out	TX=Time-out Opponent	S=Substitution Serving Team	Sx=Opponent Substitution	

If the receiving team wins the rally, it receives a point which is recorded on the line of the NEXT server's
a number and a square is drawn around it. Also draw a square around the same point on the team's running score.

Date:	Home:	Visitor:	Set #:

| Time-Outs | | Game No: | | First Serve (Check Box Below) | | | Time-Outs | | | |

Serve Order	Player No	Team:	L:			Serve Order	Player No	Team:	L:
I				1 16	1 16	I			
				2 17	2 17				
II				3 18	3 18	II			
				4 19	4 19				
				5 20	5 20				
III				6 21	6 21	III			
				7 22	7 22				
				8 23	8 23				
IV				9 24	9 24	IV			
				10 25	10 25				
V				11 26	11 26	V			
				12 27	12 27				
				13 28	13 28				
VI				14 29	14 29	VI			
				15 30	15 30				

Final Score: | Official Verification

Subs: 1 2 3 4 5 6 7 8 9 10 11 12 13 14 15 16 17 18   Subs: 1 2 3 4 5 6 7 8 9 10 11 12 13 14 15 16 17 18

Comments: ....   Comments: ....
....

Referee: ....   Umpire: ....

Scorekeeper: ....

Date:	Home:	Visitor:	Set #:

Time-Outs		Game No:		First Serve (Check Box Below)		Time-Outs		

Serve Order	Player No	Team:	L:			Serve Order	Player No	Team:	L:
I				1 16	1 16	I			
				2 17	2 17				
II				3 18	3 18	II			
				4 19	4 19				
				5 20	5 20				
III				6 21	6 21	III			
				7 22	7 22				
IV				8 23	8 23	IV			
				9 24	9 24				
				10 25	10 25				
V				11 26	11 26	V			
				12 27	12 27				
				13 28	13 28				
VI				14 29	14 29	VI			
				15 30	15 30				

Final Score: | | | Official Verification

Subs: 1 2 3 4 5 6 7 8 9 10 11 12 13 14 15 16 17 18   Subs: 1 2 3 4 5 6 7 8 9 10 11 12 13 14 15 16 17 18

Comments: ....   Comments: ....

Referee: ....   Umpire: ....

Scorekeeper: ....

Key:
- C=Playing Captain
- P-1=Penalty Point
- T= Time-out
- 1=Point
- P=Penalty
- TX=Time-out Opponent
- ⊣ =Loss of Rally
- Px=Penalty Opponent
- S=Substitution Serving Team
- ☐ =Point Scored Off Loss of Rally
- R=Reply
- Sx=Opponent Substitution
- △ =Libero Point
- Rs=Re-Serve

If the receiving team wins the rally, it receives a point which is recorded on the line of the NEXT server's a number and a square is drawn around it. Also draw a square around the same point on the team's running score.

Date: Home: Visitor: Set #:

Serve Order	Player No	Team:											L:		First Serve (Check Box Below)		Serve Order	Player No	Team:											L:	
		Time-Outs		Game No:															Time-Outs											
I															1 16 2 17	1 16 2 17	I													
II															3 18 4 19 5 20	3 18 4 19 5 20	II													
III															6 21 7 22 8 23	6 21 7 22 8 23	III													
IV															9 24 10 25	9 24 10 25	IV													
V															11 26 12 27 13 28	11 26 12 27 13 28	V													
VI															14 29 15 30	14 29 15 30	VI													
												Final Score:												Official Verification						

Subs: 1 2 3 4 5 6 7 8 9 10 11 12 13 14 15 16 17 18   Subs: 1 2 3 4 5 6 7 8 9 10 11 12 13 14 15 16 17 18

Comments: ....   Comments: ....
....

Referee: ....   Umpire: ....

Scorekeeper: ....

Key:

C=Playing Captain	1=Point	⊣ =Loss of Rally
P-1=Penalty Point	P=Penalty	Px=Penalty Opponent
T= Time-out	TX=Time-out Opponent	S=Substitution Serving Team

□ =Point Scored Off Loss of Rally   △ =Libero Point
R=Reply   Rs=Re-Serve
Sx=Opponent Substitution

If the receiving team wins the rally, it receives a point which is recorded on the line of the NEXT server's
a number and a square is drawn around it. Also draw a square around the same point on the team's running score.

Date: Home: Visitor: Set #:

	Time-Outs		Game No:			First Serve (Check Box Below)		Time-Outs			

Serve Order	Player No	Team:			L:			Serve Order	Player No	Team:			L:
I						1 16 2 17	1 16 2 17	I					
II						3 18 4 19 5 20	3 18 4 19 5 20	II					
III						6 21 7 22 8 23	6 21 7 22 8 23	III					
IV						9 24 10 25	9 24 10 25	IV					
V						11 26 12 27 13 28	11 26 12 27 13 28	V					
VI						14 29 15 30	14 29 15 30	VI					
				Final Score:							Official Verification		

Subs: 1 2 3 4 5 6 7 8 9 10 11 12 13 14 15 16 17 18   Subs: 1 2 3 4 5 6 7 8 9 10 11 12 13 14 15 16 17 18

Comments: ....   Comments: ....

....

Referee: ....   Umpire: ....

Scorekeeper: ....

Key:
C=Playing Captain	1=Point	⊣ =Loss of Rally	☐ =Point Scored Off Loss of Rally	△ =Libero Point
P-1=Penalty Point	P=Penalty	Px=Penalty Opponent	R=Reply	Rs=Re-Serve
T= Time-out	TX=Time-out Opponent	S=Substitution Serving Team	Sx=Opponent Substitution	

If the receiving team wins the rally, it receives a point which is recorded on the line of the NEXT server's
a number and a square is drawn around it. Also draw a square around the same point on the team's running score.

Date:	Home:	Visitor:	Set #:

Time-Outs		Game No:		First Serve (Check Box Below)		Time-Outs			

Serve Order	Player No	Team:	L:			Serve Order	Player No	Team:	L:
I				1 16 2 17	1 16 2 17	I			
II				3 18 4 19 5 20	3 18 4 19 5 20	II			
III				6 21 7 22	6 21 7 22	III			
IV				8 23 9 24 10 25	8 23 9 24 10 25	IV			
V				11 26 12 27 13 28	11 26 12 27 13 28	V			
VI				14 29 15 30	14 29 15 30	VI			
			Final Score:						Official Verification

Subs: 1 2 3 4 5 6 7 8 9 10 11 12 13 14 15 16 17 18   Subs: 1 2 3 4 5 6 7 8 9 10 11 12 13 14 15 16 17 18

Comments: ....   Comments: ....

Referee: ....   Umpire: ....

Scorekeeper: ....

Key: C=Playing Captain   1=Point   ⊣ =Loss of Rally   ☐ =Point Scored Off Loss of Rally   △ =Libero Point

P-1=Penalty Point   P=Penalty   Px=Penalty Opponent   R=Reply   Rs=Re-Serve

T= Time-out   TX=Time-out Opponent   S=Substitution Serving Team   Sx=Opponent Substitution

If the receiving team wins the rally, it receives a point which is recorded on the line of the NEXT server's
a number and a square is drawn around it. Also draw a square around the same point on the team's running score.

Made in United States
North Haven, CT
22 June 2023